LUMBE

G000252291

Cover: The author in action.
Overleaf: The author in her newly acquired
Women's Land Army Uniform.

LUMBER JILL

Her story of four years in the
Women's Timber Corps, 1942-45

Mavis Williams

Ex Libris Press

First published in 1994 by
Ex Libris Press
1 The Shambles
Bradford on Avon
Wiltshire

Typeset in 10 point Palatino

Design and typesetting by Ex Libris Press

Cover printed by Shires Press, Trowbridge
Printed and bound in Britain by
Cromwell Press Ltd., Broughton Gifford, Wiltshire

ISBN 0 948578 62 9

Acknowledgements
To Bette Anderson for supplying WTC insignia for reproduction here.
To the *Cornish Times* for permission to reproduce the article on pages
94-96 and to Barbara Dean for the picture on page 93 (this had
belonged to her late father, Bill Hann).
This and all the other Cornish photographs were taken by professional photographer Alan Date of Bodmin and are his copyright. The
publisher has made efforts, which have proved unsuccessful, to
contact Mr. Date to seek permission to reproduce those photographs
here.

CONTENTS

The Women's Land Army cap badge, bearing an image of a wheatsheaf, was soon replaced by that of a pine tree (below). The crossed axes were also adopted by the Women's Timber Corps and worn as an arm badge — see cover picture.

1 I join the Forestry Section of the Women's Land Army

Hello! My name is Mavis. At least, it has been for almost seventy years. I say for *almost* seventy years, for during the most memorable, the most hilarious four years of my life I was known as Tich. Why 'Tich'? Well, four feet eleven and a half inches in stockinged feet is not exactly enormous, is it? Can I tell you about those years?

It all started in 1941. Merseyside had received a pasting from the German bombers. Devastation was everywhere. My home had been blasted several times, the victim of incendiary bombs, and, with all the windows boarded up with cardboard, it was an excellent advertisement for many well-known grocery brands! My parents had moved to Wales, their business gone, while my brother was in the Navy. But what was I doing? After serving my apprenticeship as a filing clerk at twelve shillings and sixpence a week, and having worked as a telephonist and ledger clerk, I was by that time being trained as a buyer for a well-known fashion house. This held the promise of foreign travel, when all this was over. But *was* there to be a future, for me, for anyone? At nineteen years of age I would be called up anyway. Shouldn't I decide what I wanted to do, before it was decided for me? The WRNS? The ATS? The WAAF? With my training and qualifications I would probably be stuck in an office for the duration, and that was just what I wanted to avoid. I didn't want to be inside. But I was a city girl! So? It seemed as though it had to be the Women's Land Army, though quite honestly, at that time I was frightened to death of cows – and still am!

I applied in January 1942 and soon went for an interview. Four pairs of eyes, one pair belonging to a large, imposing lady, who was to do most of the talking, surveyed me from top to toe. Oh dear! Not again. I knew what was coming, for hadn't I passed the Civil Service Examination, only to fail my Medical for that vital half-inch below the then regulation minimum height. However, in the course of that interview, I was told that I would be wasted in the WLA. But, with my qualifications, there was a Corps being formed for which a slightly higher academic standard was needed. This was a new venture to be inaugurated by the Ministry of Supply in order to release able-bodied men from the forests, the saw-mills and haulage work for the Services. It had become necessary to increase the production of pit-props for our coal mines, because timber was no longer available from abroad due to shipping losses and the 'blockade'.

Would I be interested? I most certainly was!

In a few days there was the Medical at which I was told that I seemed 'strong enough'.

Then *the* parcel arrived. My uniform! I couldn't wait to try it on. Alas! The breeches came down to my ankles. Not even the thick knee socks could disguise the fact. So, off to Dad. He was a Master Tailor and alterations were soon underway. A Land Army style hat and badge had been issued as a temporary measure and I can remember striding along the prom in Torquay, head held high, thick, stiff brown shoes killing me!

I was a member of the Women's Timber Corps! Unknown then, unknown to most people now. Honestly, have you ever heard of it?

At last a Travel Warrant and instruction to travel to Suffolk arrived. Suffolk! Why that's the end of the earth! What an adventure! Change in London. The Underground! A veritable maze of routes and stations so I'd been told. Here I go!

On a cold, windy day in March 1942, I, together with 119 others, stood on a small station platform somewhere in Suffolk, all in spank-ing new uniforms. Shy glances, an occasional smile, stilted conversation, kit bags slung over shoulders, Army-style. We were shepherded, herded, into Army trucks and so began the journey to the Camp, down quiet country lanes with many a bump, twist and turn.

The first WTC Training Camp at Culford, Suffolk.

The gates of the Camp were set in high brick perimeter walls, surrounded by forests as far as the eye could see. Large wooden huts stood stark and ugly in the clearings. Maybe it would look better in the morning light, for the Assembly Hut offered little more than a hard concrete floor on which to sit.

What a welcome! Twelve to a dormitory; washing facilities in a nearby hut; rising bell 6 a.m.; P.T. 6.30 a.m.; breakfast 7 a.m.; lights outs 10 p.m.!

"No doubt you're tired after long, tedious journeys, get tidied up, then go to the Mess Hut for a meal."

Divided at random into twelves we were shown to the dormitories – spartan but adequate! After all, we each had a bedside locker and there were two open wardrobes! An air of excitement prevailed, and friendships, which have stood the test of time, began there and then. Try the beds – iron frames and palliasses; straw pillows. Rolled back,

9

the palliasses revealed three separate wooden planks resting on the rim of the iron frames.

A rather plump girl, named Daphne, stared in horror,

"I can't sleep on that!"

"You won't care what you sleep on after tomorrow," retorted one of the others. How right she was! That night the last girl into the hut jumped into bed only to go right through the middle, to land on the floor in a heap of bedclothes. The fun had started!

"You rotten lot," she shrieked.

A head bobbed up.

"I don't know what all the fuss is about. It's much more comfortable here on the floor, anyway. Try it."

The warden never did find out how many palliasses spent the night on the floor!

A bell pierced the early morning quiet, its strident message clear: Get up! One foot out of bed. It's cold! Some still sleeping. Shake them! Dash to the wash-house. Its muddy! Remember to put shoes on tomorrow, slippers are no good here! Oh! the water's cold. Pity those waiting in the queue! The morning air cut like a knife, as scantily clad girls, clutching toilet bags, towels slung over their shoulders, waited their turns. They'll learn that it is the early bird etc. with only a limited number of wash basins. Pandemonium reigns! Most, I am sure, managed only a lick and a promise, scurrying back to their huts to scramble into dungarees, put covers tidily over their beds, hopefully hiding any debris from the warden's eagle eye in case of hut inspection, then on to the field for P.T.

What a miserable group of girls gathered in the morning mist, shivering and blue with cold, eyes half-closed, some heads just released from curlers and as yet uncombed.

"Well let's be 'avin' yer."

The P.T. Instructor was a Hercules of a man, dressed in a vest and shorts. "'Ere, this ain't no church bazaar. Get yourselves spread out. Let's get movin'."

Reluctantly we moved to a chosen spot. "Right now, get them legs movin' – if you've got any under them 'orrible long pants. Runnin' on the spot, *commence!*"

"Up! Up!" he yelled, "you're not ruddy tortoises, get yer shells off. Let's see some sweat!"

For almost half an hour we jumped, ran, swayed, turned and circled. So began the process of turning us into Amazons! If Hercules had his way that wouldn't take long! Half dead, but certainly warmer, we tottered into the Mess Hut, already feeling the effects of our exertions. After about a week or so we actually enjoyed being bullied into action, and grew, as it was, 'to the manner born'.

Breakfast that first morning was a much noisier meal than supper had been.

"I've got muscles in places I shouldn't have," one girl complained, "and they all ache."

"What's the next form of torture"? asked another.

Guesses as to what the rest of the day would bring were bandied about, but no bets were taken as no one really had a clue. After the last half hour's slog, the ice had been well and truly broken!

We made our way back to the Assembly Hall and sat on the floor awaiting the arrival of the Commandante. She duly arrived with the 'Man from the Ministry', a dwarf by comparison. Dressed in a thick tweed suit, shirt and tie, lisle stockings and heavy brogues, she typified my idea of a real country woman. Surveying us over horn-rimmed spectacles below short-cropped hair, she started as she obviously meant to go on – with authority.

"Better make yourselves comfortable as this may take some time! Settled in, girls? Our first contingent! No one knows how, or if, this is going to work, but we have high hopes! This will be a six weeks' course under the auspices of the Ministry of Supply, during which those obviously not suited to or unhappy with the work can opt out. Training in all aspects of the work will be given. Aptitudes will be noted. You will be allowed some choice, then be posted to various parts of the country."

Cor, this floor's hard! Get on with it! We're all agog at the prospect of actual forestry – felling, lopping, stripping, sawing, stacking, loading, charcoal making.

"I hope you are all feeling strong," the man from the Ministry remarked. (Noises from the floor!)

"You're not? Never mind, you soon will be, if what I saw on the field early this morning is anything to go by." A hint of a smile on an otherwise dead-pan face. (Loud Groans!)

"To continue. Your work will include haulage – driving lorries and tractors, loading, unloading. You are no doubt aware that women drivers are not held in high esteem? Now is the time to prove us wrong."

"Lord High and Mighty," was heard from the back.

"To continue, if I may! Measuring is the third category – the 'office part' – calculating, recording, assessing volume, wages, correspondence, communications. You must be able to add two and two together, at least! You will also visit the local saw-mills for a short course of instruction."

Great! The first sounded exciting, but no Measuring for me, I thought. Two and two won't make four, in my case.

Divided into three groups, we piled into the waiting lorries. Away we go! To where? To the woods, of course, to the woods. The Forestry Section for me! I'm going to be a Lumber Jill!

2 At Training Camp in Suffolk and from Mavis to 'Tich'

The Suffolk terrain was very flat. Large open, sandy spaces with rutted surfaces were evident between the woods. The trees looked huge. No strangled coppice for us to start on! In one of the clearings the truck came to a halt. As we got out we saw three men waiting. They all wore breeches, thick sweaters, huge boots and looked very countrified and weather-beaten.

Mr. Davies, raising a battered trilby, introduced himself. He was a forester from Wales and his soft but obvious accent was to be mimicked on many occasions.

"Well, the first thing to do is to learn to light a fire. Can't do without our cup of tea, now can we?"

Looking round the group his eye alighted on me, perhaps because of my lack of inches.

"Right, Tich," he said, "you're to have the very important job of making tea twice today, when I've shown you all how to get started".

So Tich was born, and Tich I was to remain.

There was a pile of new axes upon which we gazed in horror, for to us they resembled instruments of torture, heavy and sharp.

"It won't take long to get the hang of it, or should I say the swing of it," Mr. Davies laughed, as he explained the knack of sliding one hand up and down the shaft, while his two colleagues demonstrated a 'V' cut into the bole of the tree.

"One horizontal, one at forty-five degrees, try to get them to meet."

All took an axe, except me.

"Go and collect some leaves and twigs, Cariad. Get the drier ones from underneath," explained Mr. Davies.

I was shown how to build a pyramid of twigs over the leaves, then I put a match to it. The smoke!

"Get on your belly, Cariad, to help it along. A few more blows will do it."

There was smoke in my eyes and up my nose, my fringe was singed, my face red with the effort. I sneezed and sneezed! The fire was alight!

That morning we had each been given a pack of sandwiches, but, in future, would have to remember to collect it ourselves – or else! Two large billy cans had also been loaded on the trucks. Forked branches were cut, one hammered into the ground on either side of the fire, the billies hung on another branch set in the forks and left until the water boiled.

Now to try my hand at felling!

Cries of "Oh! Mr. Davies, my axe is stuck," or "Hoorah! I've got a piece out," could be heard.

When the billies boiled I threw in several measures of tea. How horrible it looked with most of the tea floating on the top. A stir with a piece of stick did not improve it much.

"Coo, Tich, what did you boil in this? Kippers?"

"Old socks, more like it," were just two of the derogatory suggestions made when the gang sat round the fire with their tin mugs of tea.

"Never mind, Cariad," soothed Mr. Davies, a twinkle in his eye, "put a little piece of wood in the water next time, it absorbs the smoke and improves the flavour."

Despite floating tea leaves there were no more complaints, at least not about the tea. But lunch – that was a different matter. The rolls were stale and the cold bread and butter pudding defied description!

"I know that there's a war on, but this is ridiculous," Ruth complained, "my delicate digestion won't stand it."

"Give it to the birds," someone chimed in.

As quick as a flash Rita retorted amid laughter, "What are you, sadists? Don't you like our feathered friends? If they eat this they'll never get off the ground again!" The camaraderie was growing.

One day, while we were valiantly hacking away at the poor trees which were growing on the side of a large sandy waste, the Tank Corps arrived, complete with tanks! Clanking and creaking, the armoured monsters finally come to a stop on the edge of the wood. Earphoned heads appeared above the turrets, amazed faces broke into grins and remarks too blue to mention were hurled in our direction.

"Hi Red!" came a shout from a Corporal. "Want another hand on your axe?"

"You keep your hands to yourself, soldier," retorted Judith, the red-head.

"Aw, don't be like that. Take pity on a poor lonely soldier," he said advancing. "Come on, Red. What's you name?" he pleaded.

"It's certainly not Hood," flashed Judith.

The Corporal laughed loudly.

"No, you're not Red Riding Hood and I'm not the big, bad wolf either. I'm the lonely woodsman come to ask the lovely lady for a date."

A date? Where, doing what? Till then few of us had ventured out of the camp in the evenings, mainly because we were too tired, and our bodies were too sore from the unusual and unaccustomed exercise. Judith turned towards him. She liked what she saw.

"All right, Corporal. You're on."

"Know the village?" He asked.

"What village?"

"There's one up the road from your camp," he explained.

"Meet you in the Fox and Goose about eight."

"Fine, as long as you realise that I'm no goose for plucking."

Many of the other soldiers had followed the Corporal's lead, so that evening promised to be our first 'social' event.

The fire wouldn't burn. The kindling was damp from overnight rain. I tried every trick I knew and, so far, had managed a few puffs of smoke which disappeared as I watched them! I added some fresh twigs, then, on all fours, began to blow. A lick of flame! Keep blowing! I blew so hard that some burning ash landed on my arm.

"Oo-ow!" Before I knew what was happening, my arm was gripped firmly in two strong hands and a field dressing was applied with professional thoroughness.

"There, that should do it," said the Sergeant who was squatting beside me, patting me on the head. I looked up to thank him and saw a mass of blond curly hair spilling from beneath a black beret, a pair of bright blue eyes and a saucy grin.

We sat watching the fire burn until the billies boiled. His name was James Scott and he had been a motor engineer before his call-up. We agreed to meet that evening at the local, but as he got up and walked away I laughed to myself, for he was over six feet tall!

"He's in for a surprise, when he sees me standing!"

The Fox and Goose was the only local for miles, so obviously it was the focal point for any socialising. That evening the pub was the place where, for a few brief hours, the war could be forgotten. That is, until a young soldier named Jamie went to the bar.

"Evening landlord. What's going this evening?"

"Well son, you've two choices: beer and beer."

"I'll go for the first. What are you having girls? First choice or second choice? Beer or beer?"

"Oh, we'll have shandies please," said Rita, "good for the muscles. And boy, have I got muscles – all aching ones!"

One of the soldiers started 'tinkling' on a rather old piano and, within seconds, was besieged with demands for 'Roll out the Barrel', 'Run Rabbit Run' and many, many more, sung with fervour if not too tunefully.

"Gawd! Just look at the time," exclaimed Pat. "We've two miles to walk and we're supposed to be in by ten."

"So what!" said Judith, thoroughly enjoying herself.

"All that flaming felling. Feel my biceps," Pat remarked, rolling up her sleeves. "They're good enough to haul me over the gate."

"There's nothing wrong with my biceps, either," said Judith, "but I'm not climbing any gate!"

When we arrived back at camp some of the Staff were waiting. They shooed our escorts away, and us to our huts. However, Judith took so long saying 'Goodnight' to her soldier that she was locked out! Apparently she had to be shoved over the wall and, knowing that she would be seen if she walked up the long drive, had wriggled on her tummy over the field, unfortunately unable to avoid all the cow pats! Hut 8 was in darkness. But, when she opened the door, the smell came in with her! We held our noses and our breath for we knew what was about to happen. Yes, we'd removed the middle board of her bed.

"You rotten lot," she muttered, gingerly stripping.

As she did so, a ghostly form wrapped in a sheet picked up her offending outer garments and deposited them outside, where they remained until morning. Before we left, most of us had been caught by the bed 'trick'.

Next day the tanks returned. One by one, we girls 'disappeared'. Some of us had climbed into the turrets, fancying our chances as drivers, while others had earphones on listening to the radio. Mr. Davies, as a rule the most patient of men, was rather cross.

"What's going on here? he demanded. "Haven't you boyos got anything better to do? Don't you know there's a war on?"

He gathered us together and gave us a serious talking to.

"Now, we've got to stop hacking at these trees and fell one properly. Come here, Tich."

I moved over to a tree near which he was standing.

"Now, show us how, Tich."

Was my face red! But there was nothing for it.

I struck the base horizontally, then diagonally. The cuts met! A triangular sliver of wood flew out. Hurrah!

"Keep it up girl," urged Mr. Davies, smiling again, "You're doing fine."

He stood with his old trilby on the back of his head, encouraging every blow, as I valiantly swung the axe.

"Let the axe do the work, Cariad." To the cheers and jeers of the others the cut grew.

"Enough," said Mr. Davies. "Now get hold of the other end of this saw. We're going to saw this through, but first we must know where it is going to fall. Always downhill, if possible. Find out the direction of the wind."

We sawed. The tree gave a shudder and I called out exultantly 'TIMBER!' , as the tree fell exactly where it was meant to.

During those early days the woods resounded to girlish cries of 'Timber', often with a frantic note as a tree was about to fall in an unintended direction. Those not quick enough often had a brush with a branch – or two!

That night in the hut, talking about the day's work and the visit of the Tank Corps, I said, quite sincerely, "I don't think that I have ever experienced such a thrill in my life as when that tree came down. I'm keeping a piece of it – and dating it."

"Poor James," wailed Judith. "Tich gets more thrills from chopping down trees and dating them than dating him."

"Your trouble, Judith," I said, throwing the sock I'd been darning at her, 'is a one track mind – tank tracks!"

"I hate darning socks," I said, throwing the other one down.

"Tell you what Tich," said Daphne from her bed, "you scratch my back and I'll darn your socks."

Scratch her back?

"O.K. Daf, I'll scratch your back. You darn my socks."

And so she did.

"I'll scratch your back any time," said Judith, "If you'll darn mine too."

So, dear Daphne spent many contented hours so occupied.

"Hey." said Rita, "have any of you ever seen old Davies without his battered old trilby?"

"Never," chorused the gang.

"I wonder if he wears it in bed? I wonder if he takes a bath in it?" were some of the facetious remarks.

"Why don't you find out?" dared Mary.

"Old boyo Davies is a gentleman," Judith began, amid cries of "I should hope so. How do you know?" and gales of laughter from the others.

"He's no cradle snatcher. He must be fifty if he's a day," Judith continued when the laughter had subsided. "Anyway, I like him." So did we all.

"It's the lopping and topping that gets me," moaned Daf. "Axing all those branches off as close to the trunk as possible. The smoke gets in my eyes, in my throat and in my clothes when we burn the waste. Leaving the little bend at the top is hard too. I'm not opting for Forestry."

"Well, Daf, it your don't leave that little wave at the top you'll have the Bevan boys after you," Rita said.

Daphne looked puzzled.

"Bevan Boys! Who are the Bevan Boys?"

"They're the young men who prefer to work in the coal mines instead of being conscripted into the Services," it was patiently explained to her.

"Oh! My pit-props look wavy all the way down."

"Never mind, Daf," sympathised Judith, tongue in cheek. Perhaps you'll start a new fashion in the pits – wavy galleries!"

None of our pit-props are that good yet, anyway," placated Mary, "I'm damned if I can get a saw to go straight. It looks simple enough, but the rhythm of 'pull, pull' and no 'push, push' is so difficult. My props have curved tops."

Changing the conversation Brenda asked, "How is it that you have so much chocolate and fruit, Tich? I never see your opening a parcel."

"Some of the villagers give it to me," I answered, "I reckon they think that I need nourishment. Maybe they feel sorry for me!"

"Lucky you," Brenda grudged,"my five-feet nine-inches gets me nowhere. You even pinch the tall Tommies, too."

The warden's footsteps put an end to all conversation as the girls tumbled into bed. She never knew how many tumbled on to the floor – and stayed there for the night!

Above: Clearing a way through tangled coppice;
Opposite above: Sawing up cord wood with a bow-saw;
Opposite below: Sawing cord wood into 12" - 18" pieces, ready to stack the charcoal kiln. Note the lack of protection on the saw. The girls had not had prior training on this porta-saw.

3 Civilians become Lumber Jills

The girls soon settled into the routine of camp life – the early mornings, early nights, the occasional clandestine meetings with boy friends, a visit to the local. A few girls decided that this was not the life for them and left, but the rest formed small gangs, eventually becoming moderately skilful at both felling and making pit props. In fact, a sizeable pile was emerging, when one day I heard a sound, a sound which I had not heard since my days in the Liverpool blitz.

"Surely that was a bomb, Rita?"

"Sounded just like it," Rita whispered.

Just then Boyo Davies appeared shouting, frantically waving his arms.

"Get down on your bellies, girls. Get down!" he ordered as he suited his actions to his words. Bewildered, we all fell flat on the ground into prickly needles and branches lying around.

"What the heck is going on?" Judith called out.

Raising his head, Mr. Davies shouted back, "The b– army and the b– RAF have decided to hold a practice operation with live ammo! The b– RAF is dropping high explosive on the waste ground. No one remembered to tell me. Stay where you are. Keep your fingers and everything else crossed!"

"I hope that the Air Force know what they're doing. Their aim had better be good or 'goodbye' us," trembled Rita, with great fervour.

We were there for almost two hours, a miserable, worrying two hours amid the noise and the dust.

"It's all over, thank heaven," bellowed Mr. Davies, as an uncanny silence descended on the wood after the turmoil of the mock battle.

"My ears are buzzing," groaned Brenda, emerging through a cloud of dust.

"What did you say?" shouted Judith. "I can't hear. My ears are buzzing."

A dirty, bedraggled group of girls climbed into the lorries, lacking their usual exuberance, and with much to think about.

The next day was very wet, raining heavily and unsuitable for work in the woods. The girls were ordered to uncover a potato clamp near the cookhouse. Great! That'll make a change.

However, they were soon to discover that many of the potatoes had gone rotten and soon a most unpleasant smell emanated from the clamp. I tied a handkerchief over my nose and mouth as did many of the others.

"Oh, no!" came a shriek from Judith.

She stood, fingers dripping a thick black gunge onto her boots, but as she started to walk away she slipped and fell almost head-first into the foul heap.

"You don't exactly smell like a bed of roses," I said, as Rita and I hauled her out, trying to avoid contamination.

"Go and have a bath, before the rush starts."

For once Judith was crestfallen, her usual *joie de vivre* dampened by the sticky, black gunge.

"I never want to see a ruddy potato, let alone eat one, again," she muttered as she trudged off.

However, that night, she produced some really first class spuds. She had been to the Mess Hut before she'd had a bath. One of the cooks had taken pity on her, and to forestall any aversion to the lowly but necessary spud, had advised her to bake them on the stove in the hut. None of us was very keen after our clamp experience, but being healthy, hungry bodies we thoroughly enjoyed them, especially with the butter which had been smuggled out of the Mess.

That evening we were told that it was now time to change our work. We were to try Haulage.

However, before we started on this we were taken to see a huge sawmill which whined noisily and continuously.

"I'm terrified," whispered Rita.

"I'd never get used to that row," added Judith. "Do the men wear ear plugs?" she asked the Foreman.

"No. They get used to it. Don't reckon they even notice now." For many this was not a happy experience, but we still had to spend some time in the sawmill at the bottom end of the camp site.

As usual we left by lorry, even though the mill was not far away. The lorry deposited us in a large clearing in which were stacks of pit-props. A man in dungarees and a cloth cap was waiting for us.

"It's a change from the eternal trilby, at least," whispered Judith.

"Hello girls," he greeted us. "I'm Sid Sutton and I'm going to show you how to use the saws and handle pit-props. Then his eyes alighted on me.

"I don't believe it! Now they're sending me midgets." He thought it a huge joke and rocked with laughter. At this point Rita, who was not amused, nudged me, nodding in Sid's direction.

"What?" I asked.

"Look at his hands," she suggested.

With some difficulty I did so. He had half a finger missing on one hand and a thumb off the other.

"Oh dear", I thought to myself. "Not a very good advert for saw milling."

Ruth shivered, terrified of what was to come.

Unaware of our interest in him, Sid said, "Gather round, girls," and proceeded to lift a huge piece of wood on to the saw, which was whirling round.

"Now, watch your hands. Don't get too near the wheel."

"He hasn't always practised what he's preaching, obviously," observed Rita, shuddering as Sid pushed the wood forward.

"When you get near the end, push the last piece of wood through with another piece," we were instructed.

After a few scary, hair-raising days and some 'near misses' we were given instruction on the tractor, how to start it and drive it.

Poor Rita was the only one who couldn't start it.

"I feel such a fool. Maybe I am one," she was heard to say.

"I'll show him," I said to myself, puffing out my chest and pulling myself up to my full four-feet eleven-and-a-half-inches. Blimey, the pit props looked huge after those we'd left behind on the previous site. They were. They were nine feet long with end diameters of over nine inches!

"Three of these could weigh over a hundredweight," Sid informed us as he showed us how to lift and put them on our shoulders. Manfully we lifted, heaved them on to our shoulders and staggered towards the waiting lorry. It became easier after the first half dozen or so, but I could see that the loaders were not happy.

"Mr. Sutton," one of them called. "It's breaking my back to have to bend so low to reach Tich's props."

That was the end of me on that particular job. Tractor driving? That held a certain fascination. But you've guessed it—I couldn't reach the controls! I tried very hard, but even with my bottom perched on the very edge of the seat my legs just wouldn't stretch far enough. So – back to the Forestry group!

Having already done a fortnight I felt a little superior. I was able to show off my newly acquired skills. No longer was I the 'tea girl'.

We did have most weekends off when we washed our hair – usually in cold water, but occasionally we heated some water in a billy perched on top of the stove in our hut. If we were lucky we were taken by lorry to Bury St. Edmunds where we could go to a dance in the Corn Exchange. Because we had to catch the lorry back we never stayed to the end, and rarely had time to bid fond farewells to our partners!

There were many more visits to the local, but no lasting friendships or attachments were made with the soldiers, for most of them were on training courses and the faces which popped up from the tank turrets were often different from those that we had expected. We made our own fun in the camp, and were usually too tired anyway for much social life. One night Rita woke to terrible groans coming from occupants of several of the beds.

"Tich! Wake up!"

"What's the matter?" I said half asleep. Then I, too, heard the groans, and leapt out of bed, throwing a blanket around me. Some of the girls were obviously ill and in some pain. Clad only in my blanket I braved the dark and cold to raise Matron, while Rita and Sarah did what they could for the stricken girls.

"Cover them in blankets," ordered Matron, "and get them to the sick bay."

By that time she was receiving word that the same malady had struck other huts. Lines of blanket-clad, tousle-headed, pale-looking specimens wobbled, staggered or tottered over to the sick bay. Those of us who seemed to be all right were sent back to our huts, where we gathered round the stoves to make a cuppa as we couldn't sleep. Some time later matron informed us that most of the huts had been affected. The doctor had arrived and diagnosed some form of food poisoning, which would have to be investigated. We'd had curry for our evening meal; it appeared that those of us who had refused it were OK, so the finger pointed!

We were warned not to visit the patients and were put on Camp duties that day. However, those with beds near the windows of the overcrowded sick-bay used sign language on our illicit visits. After a couple of days it was obvious that they were starving and were beseeching us to get some food to them. So, armed with bags hidden under our overcoats, we boarded a bus to the nearest town; fortunately it was Saturday and our time was our own. The only food not rationed seemed to be fish and chips, cakes and tripe! Nothing daunted we bought as much as we could carry. Back in camp, when all was quiet, we handed our spoils through the windows to grasping hand. Ugh! Cold fish and chips! More food poisoning? Apparently not, for cold as it was, it was eaten with relish.

It was now time to do a fortnight's Measuring, but I won't dwell too long on that. Suffice to say that we learnt all about girth, cubic feet, piece work, Income Tax, wages. Figures! Figures! Figures! At last training was over. The excitement mounted, but first a stiff Medical.

Where were we going to be sent?

There was supposed to be a choice but it was noticeable that those who lived in the south were sent north and vice-versa.

A list of locations was posted.

"I say girls," an excited Judith said, "there's a gang of six wanted in Shropshire,"

"I'm on," said Brenda.

"Me too," added Ruth ungrammatically.

"Count me in" said Mary, "How about you, Tich?"

"What? With you lot?"

"Oh come on. We've only one more to find then."

"O.K, O.K. I'll chance it."

A very quiet girl, who had tended to keep herself to herself, also opted to join the group. Why, I don't know. I only hoped that she would not regret it, for Prunella Cutford-Smythe was a society beauty turned lumber jill! From now on she would be known as 'the Prune'.

Before leaving Camp we were issued with green berets, brown Timber Corps badges and crossed axes for our sleeves. We really were lumber jills! We were on our way. Or should I say that we were being loosed on an unsuspecting public!

Above: Firing a kiln from a stack of crooked cord wood.
Opposite above: Civilian workers filling a charcoal kiln prior to packing it.
Opposite below: Lumber jills stacking timber. The 'figures' on the ends show the number of inches cut for piece work payments.

4 To Edgton in Herefordshire and my first Posting

Six spruce, excited young ladies stepped out of the train at Liverpool Street Station and made their way by Underground to Paddington, having already been subjected to curious glances from fellow passengers and, in fact, some doubtful remarks. We didn't care. We were proud of our uniforms. We were Lumber Jills. Our travel instructions had been explicit, but on looking at the train times we found what we thought to be a quicker combination of trains to our destination.

"We can give the place the 'once over' if we get there earlier than we are expected," suggested Judith.

There were no porters about, but what did we want a porter for? Judith spotted a trolley and appropriated it with aplomb. Luggage and kit bags were piled high. Then Rita and I found ourselves alone!

"Look, Tich," she said, "you push from behind while I guide you from the front."

Guide was the operative word, for I couldn't see over the pile, but with Ruth already pulling at the front I had to go, much to the amusement of other travellers – most of them servicemen – and to our friends' disgust who pretended not to know us. However, they soon turned up when the luggage had been stowed on the racks!

"Where the heck have you been?" Rita demanded angrily. "Anyone would think that we were the only ones with luggage."

Alas, she was to get even angrier, for after changing trains the journey soon became a nightmare. It definitely was *not* a quicker route. On the contrary, we seemed to be travelling all over England! The train stopped at every opportunity, station or no station, and every successive station seemed smaller than the last. Mary looked queasy but assured us that it was only a bout of homesickness. The rest of us had our noses pressed against the dirty windows.

"It's the back of beyond," Brenda moaned. Gloom reigned. Philosophically, the Prune said, "We can take it!" Suddenly there was a yell from Judith. "This is it! Craven Arms. We're here."

Luggage was thrown out and we tumbled out, but before we had time to stretch weary limbs a stern voice demanded, "Where on earth have you been? You should have arrived two hours ago. Why weren't you on the right train?"

The Divisional Welfare Officer was not pleased! What a start! We exchanged sheepish glances and then volunteered some lame excuses. Now more subdued, we got into his small van. The town quickly disappeared, giving way to lanes, hemmed in by tall hedges and trees. Little was said as daylight dwindled but all looked thoughtful, anxious, or both!

After what seemed miles and a steady pull up a very long hill, the van stopped at a small school building. It overlooked the village, which, as far as we could see, consisted of about twenty cottages and, as we were later to discover, a tiny shop-cum-Post Office and a local. A small, elderly, grey-haired lady opened the door. Her face was lit by her smile as she hopped out to greet us. She was the village Headmistress, reigning over a school of all ages, from five to fourteen. Children came from the adjacent villages, some walking three or four miles each way.

Rita and I shared a bedroom, the camp bed being allotted to me, as I was nearer the ground than Ruth anyway! The place was spotless, our 'landlady' sweet.

"I must tell you, girls," she said apologetically, " that all the water we use has to be brought from the communal well in the village."

That, of course, was down the hill! Talk about lumber jills, it was more like Jack and Jill! To begin with we ran down the hill and then tried to run back up again but found that by the time we reached the digs we'd lost half the water!

"I reckon," said Judith, "that our tactics are all wrong. We'll get a couple of long branches, put them across our shoulders, hang a bucket on each and climb the hill more slowly."

Imagine it! Regular baths, of course, were out of the question, so it was a case of washing down as far as possible, then up as far as possible. Once, and only once, we filled a copper boiler. It took us all evening carrying water, and then we had to sit in a zinc hip bath in front of the kitchen fire!

The woods were some distance away. When we saw where we were to work, Brenda took one look and said, "Gawd! What are we supposed to be? Ruddy hedgehogs?"

Most of the wood had been felled, but nothing had been cleared! The lopped tops and branches were covered in brambles and weeds.

"Let's go it to it, girls," yelled Judith, attacking the nearest patch of brambles with her bill-hook. We hacked and we hacked until we could pull out all the discarded branches and there was a clearing big enough to build a fire, to burn the brushwood. No guesses as to who should start the fire! Scratches galore from the brambles; itches galore from the ants and midges that had been lying in wait! But we were tough, weren't we? When the sun or fire grew too hot we stripped down to sun tops or bras.

Many of us got very sunburnt so we learned the hard way, covering up when the sun was at its height. Our path back lay over a long meadow, through a gap down which we slid on our bottoms, helping each other up if necessary, beside a steam and then into the fields bordering the village. One day, at the bottom near the gap, we found a horse which had just given birth to a foal. Rita was most concerned as the horse was on its side while the foal was struggling to stand up on its spindly legs.

"Oh," exclaimed Rita. "What shall we do about this?" I hadn't a clue, being a city girl, but said, "Let's wait for a few minutes to see if the horse gets up."

We waited and sure enought the horse struggled to its feet; the foal, still wet and slimy, tottered to suckle.

"Should we tell anybody, do you think?" queried Rita.

"Who do we tell?" I replied, for there was not a farm or building of any sort in sight.

We decided that we'd continue back to our digs and take a look in the morning. By then all that remained was a shrivilled after-birth!

Our path back was over fields, then through the village. As we approached, doors opened and we were met with incredulous stares.

"What's wrong with us?" asked Mary.

It must be admitted that we were no glamour girls, with tousled hair, red faces from the sun and wind, dungarees rolled up to our knees, coats slung over our shoulders and often singing as we walked. Perhaps we offended the local villagers' idea of modesty?

"They've never seen city creatures before," said Judith.

"I'll really give them something to stare at one of these days," came unexpectedly from the Prune, our dashing society beauty.

She had a very full wardrobe, mostly vividly coloured, and was an expert horsewoman. One evening, after supper, 'the apparition' appeared! She wore cherry-coloured slacks, a yellow sweater and a green corduroy hacking jacket topped by a multi-coloured scarf!

"I'm going riding," she announced.

Near by was a large house which, so we were told, had belonged to 'Clive of India', and was surrounded by parkland. It had been taken over by the Army for men who were not fit for overseas service. We had seen some horses galloping round so thought that the Prune was probably going there.

But, unbeknown to us, on one of her excursions to the village, she had arranged to borrow a horse. Half an hour or so later there was a shout from Brenda, "Hey, girls, the Prune's back." We crowded the door. Sure enough there was the Prune on a horse. A big, old cart-horse! You can imagine the sensation it must have created in a place where the arrival of the baker's or butcher's vans was the highlight of the week. She was quite at ease, seemingly oblivious to the row we were making and the remarks thrown at her. Most evenings she borrowed this carthorse and went for an amble. But that was not exciting enough for the Prune. The next thing we knew she was trying to get the poor animal to jump fallen trees. Often she went headlong, much to our amusement, but she calmly remounted and tried again.

Somehow the farmer had heard of her exploits. As she was rubbing the horse down one evening, a burly cloth-capped man strode up, confronting the Prune.

"Hi, girl," he bellowed angrily, "What the b– do you think you've been doing? No wonder the hoss doesn't work properly! It's losing weight! Don't you dare come near me again. Ruddy foreigners. If I'd wanted a jumper I'd 'ave bought one."

The Prune's apologies fell on deaf ears, as he furiously led his poor horse away. Nothing daunted, the Prune contacted a former Riding Stables, so was then in her element – her beautiful, long blonde hair streaming behind her as she rode.

But that was the Prune. She did some crazy things at times and delighted in doing so. One day we walked the eight miles into Craven Arms, the Prune wearing her father's Sam Browne, swinging her crop in her hand and looking like a rainbow in her multi-coloured jacket, sweater and red trousers, her blonde hair tied in a colourful bandeau. Had we been nearer civilisation all heads would have been turned but the few late shoppers in this small town did not appear to notice. Naturally, at the dance that evening, the Prune was the centre of attention.

After a day's work we were ravenously hungry. The table was always immaculately laid with white linen serviettes in silver rings and flowers. Our dear, sweet landlady had been cooking only for herself for so long that she had no idea just what we could consume. What we did have was beautifully served, but it was not enough! After every meal we took it in turns to scrape out dishes while she was in the kitchen. Ruth always volunteered to make the custard, for otherwise it was like water! Although we appreciated the faultlessly laid table we would gladly have forgone the decorations for an enamel plate laden with plenty of 'grub' after a hard day's labour!

On Sunday, Mrs. B. always sat at the head of the table, and after grace the ritual of carving the joint began. She would carefully carve one slice, then cut it in half, then the halves into half again. At first, we gazed fascinated while she did it for she was so engrossed. All the little pieces were arranged neatly round the edge of a plate! The vegetables were then put in the centre! We never questioned this procedure but thought that it was either good for our digestions, or, that way, it looked more.

The school formed part of the house or vice-versa. One large room was divided into two by a short curtain, each class able to see the legs of the children sitting in the adjoining class. Mrs. B., as Headmistress, took one class, while an uncertificated assistant took the other. Most of the children who had to come some miles to school brought sandwiches for lunch, while a drink was provided from a large, heavy, old black kettle which was constantly kept on the boil on a stove in the corner. A monitor kept the stove going with pieces of wood, also piled in a corner.

One day, it transpired, she asked Dennis, an older pupil, how his mother managed to feed her Land Girls. He must have given her some valuable advice for, after the evening meal next day, we actually sat back full, dishes unscraped on the table! An audible sigh of obvious relief escaped her, no doubt thinking to herself, "I've managed to fill you hungry so-and-so's at last!" For all her eccentricities we loved her so we took the utmost care not to say or do anything that might hurt her.

We had been there about a month when Mary's mother decided to pay her a visit if she could find accommodation and transport.

"My Mum wants to come and see me," Mary told Mrs. B., "but I have no idea where she can stay, for the hotel is eight miles away."

"Hotel accommodation, my dear! Why hotel accommodation?" questioned Mrs. B. "Your mother is most welcome here. I'll find room for her."

There was certainly no spare space in Mary's room and none anywhere else!

"I've got a camp bed spare," went on Mrs. B., "and now I have a perfectly legitimate excuse to put it on the landing. I've always wanted to sleep on the landing!"

And so she did. Nothing we could do or say would shake her. It was bad luck if someone wanted to spend a penny in the downstairs outdoor 'loo', for it either meant climbing over the recumbent Mrs. B. or bottling it! When Mary's mother had gone, Mrs. B. confessed that it had been somewhat draughty, but such was her old world charm and courtesy that her visitor's comfort was paramount!

As we had been starved of any sort of entertainment, we decided, Ruth and I, that we would go the eight miles into town, hopefully to a dance. Dear Mrs. B. offered us her ancient cycle but we couldn't find another one. "Never mind," said Rita, "one can sit on the seat while the other stands up and pedals!"

Going into town was fine, for from the village we could free-wheel for a couple of miles or so.

Dances and whist drives were held in a hall attached to the largest hotel. Nearby there was a Training School for Army Officers so partners abounded, our breeches attracting saucy remarks and other attention! We thoroughly enjoyed ourselves but the thought of the eight miles ahead of us soon dampened our spirits. Two Cadets, one the son of a Lord, accompanied us for part of the way, before branching off to their own camp. They had pointed out a 'shorter way, not as hilly'. We should have known better after the experience of the 'quicker' train! The night was dark, the lane narrow, hedges rising tall on either side, lit only by myriad glow-worms.

"Spooky, isn't it?" whispered Ruth, pushing the old bike.

Suddenly the silence was broken by, "Who goes there?" barked out by two camouflaged soldiers who jumped out of the hedge ahead of us.

"Blimey! What now?" Rita looked somewhat alarmed, "I haven't got my Identity Card!"

Quickly I slipped her mine, while I clutched my Medical Card.

"You go to one. I'll go to the other," I muttered, hopeful that neither would see both cards bearing the same name and address. "Your Identity Card," the nearest soldier demanded.

"Sorry," I said sweetly, "but I only seem to have my Medical Card. Will that do?"

"Where's your Identity Card?" he persisted.

"I must have left it in my other uniform."

All appeared to be going well, until I heard the other soldier ask Ruth something about Liverpool. She came from Essex! I grabbed my Medical Card, stepped smartly over in her direction to help her out. After being well and truly told off about my lack of identity we were allowed to continue our trek.

"Quick," urged Rita, "Let's get going before they twig something."

Up hill! Puffing, pushing, panting! We couldn't have gone more than a mile or so when we heard voices again! Hearts in our mouths we answered the "Who goes there?", hoping that these soldiers had never heard of Liverpool.

"Fingers crossed," whispered Rita.

As they approached we recognised them as Home Guards. One of them peered at us.

"Ah! they're only them timber fellers from up the school 'ouse in the village. Stayin' there, they are."

Relief! Apparently, we had been in the middle of a combined Army and Home Guard exercise!

"Who ever thought of this lark?" moaned Rita. "We want our heads testing. We don't know where we are, and how far we've yet to go."

Looking at a watch, with the aid of a match, we saw that it was already after 2 a.m. Riding and walking alternately, we pressed on. Then in the distance we saw a faint light swinging to and fro.

"What's that?" I whispered to Rita.

"Gawd knows," she replied, "but whatever it is, it's getting nearer. Someone's coming. Listen!"

We stopped. Plaintively came, "Rita! Mavis! where are you?"

We realised that it was our dear old Mrs. B.

"Thank goodness, I've found you," she almost sobbed, a coat thrown over her nightdress, hair dishevelled.

"Oh! Mrs. B.," Rita murmured throwing her arms round her, "Are we glad to see you!"

Arms round each other we continued 'home' – only a further two hundred yards or so. Apparently she couldn't sleep knowing we were still out and, as time went on, without waking the others she had lit her battered storm lantern, thrown a coat over her shoulders and had braved the intense dark and the chilly early hours.

No recriminations! This incident obviously endeared her to us more than ever, but all good things must come to an end. Our job of clearing in readiness for re-afforestation was nearly finished! Soon we heard that we were to be split up and posted to different sites. Fortunately Rita and I were to be together.

With deep regret, we packed our kit bags, and with scarcely a dry eye we bade a fond farewell to our dear old Mrs. B. We could only hope that we had given her something in return for all that she had given us, unstintingly!

5 To Forden, near Welshpool

All we knew was that we were to be transferred to another village which happened to be on the border of England and Wales. After the hospitality and kindness we had received at our last digs we couldn't help but wonder what our next billet would be like. Six of us bubbly girls waited expectantly for our promised transport. Imagine our surprise when a farm cart pulled by an ancient cart-horse lumbered up and stopped in the lane. The driver turned a wrinkled face topped by a battered trilby towards us and grunted,

"Get yourselves on this cart, best yer can."

We piled on our luggage and tried to make ourselves comfortable but space was short. Mrs. B. waved us out of sight. Up hill and down dale plodded the old horse, while the driver sat immobile – or so it seemed – as the horse made its own way.

"Well, girls, might as well have a kip; 'cause at this rate it'll be tomorrow before we get to wherever we are heading," said Ruth.

"More like next week," added Doreen trying to make a nest amid the kit-bags. We had just about settled down when we came to a stop.

"Get yourselves down with all that rubbish you got there. I've got to get back to me bed."

We sprang up expectantly only to shrink back with horror as the scene before us unfolded. A rickety, wooden gate swung loose at the end of a rutted, muddy path leading from a large, crumbling, stone-built farm-house.

"Lordee!" exclaimed the Prune. "A touch of luxury wouldn't you agree? A veritable manor-house."

Wrinkling up her nose Joan asked, "Got your swimming togs? We'll need them to get up that drive when it rains, I reckon."

Somewhat deflated, wondering what was to come, we unloaded, dumping our kit bags on the few blades of grass.

Then the apparition appeared. A very large apparition! Dressed in a long apron and wellies, a scarf tied under her chin, arms akimbo, our new landlady greeted us with,

"Took yer time, didn't yer? Expected yer hours ago. Better come in tough. Mind 'ow yer go. Don't stand on ceremony 'ere."

More whisperings, but we picked up our luggage determined to make the best of what looked to be more than a disappointment. We stepped in the door. What a shambles! The kitchen was huge and stone-flagged. In the middle was a long table cluttered with a miscellaneous assortment of pots, pans, boxes, ladles, unwashed dishes and uneaten food. This dominated an otherwise almost empty room. Cooking was obviously done on an ugly kitchen range which, a long, long time ago, may have seen some black lead. A large kettle hung on a chain over an open, recessed log fire. At least the hiss of the steam was welcoming!

"Wanna go home," whispered Doreen.

"Let's go on strike," suggested Joan.

"Maybe the food's good," came hopefully from the Prune, surveying the scene of near dereliction from under her long blonde hair.

"Follow me!" commanded the apparition, opening a door at one side of the kitchen to reveal a narrow, wooden flight of stairs. Quick march! Up we went.

"Don't know who'll sleep with who. Yer'll 'ave to sort that out among yer own selves," the apparition informed us. "Three of yer in 'ere in this 'ere room," she pointed, "Two of yer in the next room, and one of yer in the small room."

With that she left us stomping down the stairs.

"Sleep together?" queried Joan, appalled at the thought. "We were told that we would have our own beds."

We looked into the room which was to sleep three of us. The bed, covered in brown blankets, looked scruffy, but worse – it could not have been more than four feet wide! The small room? It was like a prison cell, but perhaps not as big! A shelf had been erected on one side wall, which was about five feet long and on which there was a palliasse, a pillow and a couple of rough brown blankets. We looked at one another, hardly able to believe our own eyes.

"Only one thing is certain," declared Rita. "The only one who'll go on that is Tich. Let's try it for size." With that I was hoisted unceremoniously, squirming to no avail, on to the shelf.

"There you are, tailor-made," giggled the Prune as I stretched out to my full four-feet eleven-and-a-half-inches. There was perhaps an inch to spare, if I didn't flex my feet!

By this time it was beginning to get dark but there was no sign of an oil lamp and we hadn't a torch between us, and furthermore we had no real idea of where we were.

Doreen was what could be described as a big girl, fat with it. She'd take almost the whole of the smaller bed, so for her it had to be a share of the double bed. The remaining four tossed pennies as to who would sleep with who and where!

"If Doreen sleeps in the middle there won't be any room left at the sides for us, " complained Joan. "We'll be pushed out when she turns over."

"It's not my fault if I have more meat on my bones than you lot," she said, obviously feeling uncomfortable and hard done by.

"Rita is the smallest. Let her sleep in the middle. At least she won't fall out."

"No, but I'll be even smaller squashed between you two," answered Rita.

So a somewhat heated discussion continued until, eventually, it was suggested that there should be a practice run. Fully clothed, the three jumped on the bed – with hindsight a silly thing to do as it could have collapsed – and stretched out side by side. The bed was 'overhung'.

"If you up there want anything to eat you'd best get yourselves down 'ere quick," came a bellow from downstairs.

We were ravenous! A down-cast, rather dejected 'sextet' of would-be lumber jills clumped down the stairs and sat round the kitchen table, still somewhat a mess but less cluttered.

"It'll probably be all dried up, but it'll 'ave to do," announced the apparition, taking a large, soot-encrusted pot from the range. She ladled out what appeared to some sort of brown stew, unceremoniously setting a plateful before each of us.

We got stuck in; perhaps it was because we were so hungry it tasted quite palatable and was washed down with water.

By gingerly feeling our way through the undergrowth we visited the loo which was in a hut with a door swinging on its hinges; then we were handed three candles 'to light us to bed.'

As quickly as possible we undressed one by one, as there wasn't room to undress *en masse,* and got under the old brown blankets.

"Sweet dreams!" came from the Prune.

On my shelf I slept quite well, but most of the others had a very disturbed night, Doreen finishing up on the floor after rolling out of bed twice. Rita was then able to stretch out a bit.

Needless to say our dilemma was discussed over and over again as we trekked to the woods, armed with dry bread and cheese for lunch. We decided that if we didn't sleep we couldn't work, so a complaint was made to the Foreman who contacted someone. Within a few days we were moved to other digs, but in twos, not as a 'gang'. We did at least find out on one of our evening jaunts that half the village was in England so the pub in that part of the village was open – *on Sunday!* We were to work in the same wood mainly making pit props but would only see one another at work. I would miss the Prune.

Fortunately our stay here was short as Rita and I were soon posted to a little village near Welshpool.

We could hardly believe our eyes when we saw our new digs for the first time. Leading to the imposing house was a long, winding

drive edged by fields up which we humped our luggage. Again it
was spotlessly clean, but our landlady, in contrast to Mrs. B., was a
rather plump, fresh-complexioned woman.

At one time this house had been a Hall built by a gentleman for
his seven daughters, but most of it had been destroyed by fire years
ago. There were no 'mod cons', but at least the hand water-pump was
in the courtyard just outside the back door, with a 'bucket' loo nearby.
Cooking was done on a modern type of oil-burning stove and the
'grub' was really good and wholesome, for our new landlady had
been a cook for a number of years for various 'gentry'. What im-
pressed me most was that our landlady always put on a clean, fresh
overall in which to cook.

In order to get to the wood we had to pick up a lorry in the village
– a distance of some two miles – by 7.30 a.m. As we only had the
one cycle between us, again it was one on the saddle while the other
pedalled, hoping that the village policeman was still in bed! The lorry
arrived full of workmen who had been picked up from distant
villages. As there was only a half-hood, on a wet day we were packed
like sardines, sitting on proffered knees!

The lorry picked us up outside the village pub and, depending
on the weather – and the driver – was often late. One morning Rita
and I arrived just after seven o'clock. The front door opened to reveal
the landlady in her bedroom slippers.

"Come on in out of the cold," she invited us. "I'm sure you'd feel
better for a good meal inside you" she continued, as she proceeded
to cut a thick slices of home-cured bacon from a huge piece which
hung from the ceiling of the Public Bar. With it came fried bread with
at least two eggs. We were served in her back room which was
comfortable and warm. Rita and I looked at each other wondering
what to do as food at our digs was good and adequate. We decided
that if this was to be a daily ritual that we would walk to work, hoping
that we'd walk off some of our first breakfast!

As we got to know the locals better we learned that our landlady and the landlady at the pub were 'at daggers drawn'. The pub landlady was sure that the awful woman at the Hall could not possibly feed us properly. We kept any paper bag we came across to take with us in the morning so that we could put what we couldn't eat in it, so not hurt the pub landlady as she was only being kind and mother-ly to us. Some of the others who were not so well fed welcomed the fat bacon sandwiches from our tatty little bags!

For days on end we sawed and stacked pit-props, mostly of pine and larch, both of which are very resinous woods. Our hands got sticky and very, very dirty.

"They say you've got to eat your fill of muck before you die," commented Ruth one day as we opened our sandwiches, "so here goes."

For a change, one day the Foreman handed Rita and me a bucket of whitewash and a brush each.

He told us that he wanted every tree in the wood marked with a cross as "those b– fellers are booking in more trees than they are cutting down, so Head Office wants 'em counted." Rita and I looked at each other in consternation for there were hundreds, nay thou-sands of them, set on a hillside.

"Why pick on us?" Rita asked me.

"I don't know," I replied. "Maybe we look more honest than the rest." We began to climb the hillside counting and marking each tree as we went.

The going was not easy because of the scrub undergrowth and many a time we caught our feet on outgrowing roots and ivy and, in parts, loose shale. All seemed to be going well until I heard a shout.

"Tich! Tich! Save me!"

Looking round quickly I saw Rita rolling down the loose shale towards a huge hollow in the ground.

"Grab a tree!" I yelled.

This was possibly not as easy as it sounded, for when she slipped Rita had up-ended her bucket of whitewash so was covered in the slimy liquid! I wish that I had had a camera, to snap the white ball as it rolled downhill. Fortunately Ruth managed to grab some of the coppice to check her fall feet just from the hollow. That ended the day's work! We slowly made our way back to the clearing to the raucous laughter and rude remarks from the other workers. In helping Rita I got a lot of whitewash on my clothing too, so we must have looked like ghosts emerging from the shade of the trees.

We were introduced to piece-work so, by putting our backs into it, Rita and I could earn far more than our standard weekly wages of two-pounds six-shillings.

"At this rate I'll be able to buy some new 'frillies'," I rejoiced. "They wear out so quickly at this lark. Don't know where we'll get them, though."

"In the village shop?" laughed Rita.

"I expect we'll have to wait till we get leave. Rags till then. Riches after."

"I've a whacking big hole in the sole of one of my shoes," moaned Rita, "that's another seven and a tanner gone!"

Because of our lack of funds we decided to work extra hard for a few days in order to earn some more money on piece work so that we could go to Shrewsbury on our next weekend off. We managed to get a lift most of the way so, having saved on fares, we booked into the local YWCA for a night. As we were walking over the river bridge we were stopped by two Americans who had only just arrived in this country. They wanted to know what our uniform represented. We explained to them; they were extremely interested and being ardent collectors they asked if they could buy our WLA badges as we had not yet been issued with our green berets and WTC badges. They offered us ten shillings each for them, but of course we refused. After chatting from some time we continued our walk, browsing round the shops. To our surprise we came across an old curio shop which sold all kinds of military badges and regalia. There sitting in the window were WLA hat badges priced 1/6d! We kicked ourselves for we had missed the chance of making a cool 8/6d each, more than a day's pay. We then decided to have our photographs taken.

"I'm just going to get tidied up a bit," said Rita as we approached a public loo. As your hat is in better shape than mine can I borrow it please?"

"Sure," I replied.

I happened to be standing outside a poulterer's and on impulse went inside and asked if they had a large feather. Obligingly, they gave me a pheasant's tail feather. When Rita was ready she took my hat and put it on. On the pretext of straightening it up a little I stuck the feather in the hat band. She didn't notice it even though I wore the hat with it in after her. This was, of course, against WLA rules.

Paying thirty shillings for digs normally left little over for luxuries. Only our 'top' clothes were issued, and these had to be in a pretty tattered state before replacements were forthcoming.

Our 'digs' was virtually on a main road, though a couple of miles from the village. Most evenings we walked to the 'local' to play darts and skittles with the villagers. 'Cherryade' was our main tipple, much to the amusement of the locals, but if we hadn't stuck to that we'd have been tight every night, such was their generosity.

One evening, we invited our landlady to come down the pub with us. She accepted with alacrity, as for her this was quite a treat.

"I only drink stout and port," she informed us amicably.

"Hope you're flush," whispered Rita, "I've got less than a quid."

It was an expensive way to spend an evening, but so pleased were her friends to see her that she was stood as much as she could drink. Too much! On the way back she insisted on walking on the white lines in the middle of the road and, as she always walked with a stick because of a slight limp, this was practically impossible. Progress was slow, for she weaved her way from side to side, singing happily, 'Twinkle, Twinkle, Little Star', often repeating the same line over and over and over again. Rita and I walked behind her, heaving her bulk into a near upright position at the first sign of a stumble, and edging her in the right direction. We had to literally push her up the stairs and roll her on to her bed, where, as far as we knew, she remained fully clothed all night. Unbelievably, when we came down for breakfast next morning, she showed no ill effects.

"How are you feeling this morning?" Rita asked her.

"Fine. Why shouldn't I be?" She'd either forgotten the events of the previous evening or wouldn't admit them.

Arriving home one evening we found no meal ready, which was unusual. No sign of our landlady either! At that time two of her grandchildren were staying with her as there was illness in their home.

"Where's Grannie?" I asked the nine-year-old.

"Don't know," she began to sob, "she's been gone for hours and hours."

"Have you had anything to eat?" asked Rita kindly.

"I cut some bread for Rob – and buttered it," she said between sobs.

"I want Gan-Gan," yelled Robin.

We cradled them in our arms to comfort them and promised them supper in bed. After washing their tear-stained faces, Rita and I cleaned up, then went in search of food. Nothing but bread and butter and some fat! Of course, we remembered, she always locked the food cupboard.

"Those kids can't have only bread and butter again," Rita asserted, "what the devil can we give them?"

"I know!" I exclaimed. "If she has been out all day, the eggs can't have been collected. Fried eggs?"

"Brilliant" agreed Rita.

Gingerly, I opened the gate of the hen run. Immediately they converged from all directions seeking their food. As I bent down to collect the eggs which were visible, I had fluttering birds on my back, on my head, taking a crafty peck at my bare hands. Beasts! Beating a hasty retreat, I bore the eggs triumphantly into the kitchen.

"Been dragged through a hedge?" Rita asked smugly.

"They're beasts," I replied, "beasts!"

Eggs and bread were fried in the fat, and taken to the children who were sitting up in bed expectantly,

"Don't like eggs," announced Robin.

"Come on," said Rita placatingly, "I'll tell you a story while you eat. All about a little Red Hen."

"Gan-Gan's are white." prevaricated Robin.

"I know," said Rita patiently, "but there are red ones too, and they all lay the same coloured eggs, brown or white."

"What colour was mine?" insisted Robin.

"Brown," answered Rita. "Now be a good boy and eat up before they go cold."

Rita's patient persuasion won my admiration. After several stories and many questions she tucked them in, and crooned them to sleep.

By this time we were ravenous, so more eggs and fried bread were cooked.

"What do we do now?" asked Rita. "We can't leave the kids alone."

"We'll wait for a couple of hours, then one of us will have to try to contact the village bobby. Toss you who goes."

We busied ourselves tidying up, when Rita called from the window.

"Look! Look, Tich!"

Up the drive she came – rolling, her hat shoved on the back of her head.

"I'sh tight," she informed us needlessly, eyes rolling. We sat her down. She gave us the key to the food cupboard, then immediately fell asleep.

A similar thing happened one weekend. Rita and I had strolled down to the village, but on our return, just before lunch, she was missing.

"Not again," muttered Rita, thinking of the last disappearance. We waited, but as there was no sign of her we searched the garden, the loft, the house, in case she had fallen or passed out. Nowhere! So another make-shift meal. It began to rain heavily; her coat was still in the hall. Just as we had decided that we ought to report her disappearance, up the drive she limped, sober but soaking wet, her best silk dress like an extra skin.

"I caught the bus into town," she informed us.

"There I bumped into a very old friend so we had a drink or two for old times' sake. I'm not tight you know!"

"Thank heaven for that," murmured Rita.

"I've lost my shopping bag. I had it in the pub with me, I'm sure. It's not on the bus either for I waited for it to come back." Two hours' wait!

Shortly after that incident I was promoted so had to leave Rita to her tender mercies. Soon I heard that Rita had been moved, for while drunk her landlady had knocked her down and given her a black eye. Pity! The grub was good.

6   Promoted to Ganger

Now I was to travel about alone. I was appointed as a Ganger to twenty girls – rookies – in a little place outside Hereford. This was a surprise present for my twentieth birthday as I had only been in the Corps for about four months. Again, my billet was to be an isolated cottage which, from the outside, looked like everyone's dream, for the whitewashed walls were covered by muti-coloured creepers and fantrained peach trees. At the end of the garden was a cage housing two gorgeously-feathered parakeets and was a riot of colour – wild perhaps, but spectacular. The bordering orchard contained apple, plum and damson trees. Past the parakeet cage was the primitive loo, a bucket and 'chuck it' arrangement. In the plank of wood, which served as a seat, there were two holes about two feet apart. Why? the mind boggled!

Low-beamed ceilings were a feature of the inside; the stairs bare, steep and narrow, led to a landing bedroom. Unfortunately the walls were covered with flaking, once-yellow whitewash, and dust was evident everywhere! I was to have a side bedroom with bare floor, an old wardrobe and a marble-topped washstand with basin and jug. The ancient wooden hand-pump outside provided the water which had to be carried upstairs in a bucket. When the outside pump was frozen, the ice on the top of the metal water butt had to be broken. This water was brick red in colour and, as I found when I washed my hair, harboured many tiny creatures, which had to be combed out. White undies became a paler shade of pink! Hot water from the large black kettle was only allowed at the weekend.

My landlady was small, thin and rather gaunt. Her hair was pulled severely back from her face and she usually dressed in black with a dirty white apron over her frock. Her husband, who rarely removed his cap even in the house, was also small and thin, diabetic and very hen-pecked as he couldn't answer back due to a bad stammer. All the cooking was done without the addition of salt. Shades of Camp! The potatoes! Caterpillars in the greens were a common occurrence, so it was either a case of putting them on the side of the plate or going hungry. I learnt to live with them! Slops from a tea cup were thrown on to the fire, emitting a cloud of smoke or ash. Bending down to pick up a spoon I found that all the fluff was brushed under the old-fashioned sofa. There was a mountain of it! The only oil lamp was kept in the kitchen so it was a candle to light me to bed – and this was often blown out by the draughts!

Every Sunday morning there was the ritual of taking out her best clothes, smelling of mothballs, to go to church. From her remarks on her return I gathered that it was the highlight of her week, for it gave her a chance to catch up on the gossip!

"Mrs.– was wearing a felt hat! Too warm yet! The rest of us had straws!" or "Mrs.–'usband's only been dead three months and she's wearing light stockings already! Irreverent, I call it!" Or, "Bob –, in the Air Force, brought a girl home this week! A foreigner! Such nice girls round here too. Shame!" The conversation was nothing if not one-sided.

Most of the rest of the week was spent nagging her husband. Listening to her embarrassed me and I often longed to go to his defence. Fortunately he was a very placid man. When I had been there a few weeks my landlady decided to have another lodger, a Land Girl. A single bed was rigged up in my room and I quite looked forward to having some company. Sad to relate, when she did arrive, she too, had an impediment – a cleft palate! Conversation of an intelligible nature was practically impossible. At the table it went something like this:

Land girl: "A-n-oer-u-o-eeese."

Landlady: "Pardon, Miss–?"

Landlord: "Sh-sh-shh-she wan-wa-wants a–."

Land girl: "A-n-oer-u-o-eese."

Landlady: "Pardon Miss–?"

Land girl: (impatiently, handing her cup) "A-n-oer-u-o-e-eese."

Slops were thrown into the fire and another cup of tea poured!

Apart from writing letters or reading, which with a candle were tedious, there was little to do but go to bed. But one evening the Land Girl returned from the distant inn particularly garrulous. To alleviate the situation I went up to bed, undressed quickly and feigned sleep. As usual she sat on the edge of her bed, put her voluminous flannelette nightdress over her head, and began her nightly struggle to undress under the 'tent'! I could hear her muttering to herself but when she finally got into bed I thought we were settled for the night. But no! Up she got.

"I 'ust 'ash me neck," she mumbled and proceeded to splash water over the back of her neck. This over, she returned to bed, but a few minutes later I was disturbed by a long drawn out, "Ou-Ou-Ou." I opened my eyes to see her standing on her bed, pointing to the ceiling. "Ou-Ou-Ou-Ou."

Patience exhausted, I got up to investigate and saw a poor, inoffensive spider. Opening the window I put it out, but sleep that night was haunted by spiders as big as elephants!

It seemed as though my rest was doomed not only by the Land Girl, but by my landlady's sons, both of whom had been called up, one to the Army, the other to the Navy. Although they were now used to a more liberal way of life, their mother insisted that they were in by 10 p.m. and refused them a key. The rattle of gravel on my window wakened me about midnight. Going to the small window I saw John outside. By signs he indicated that he wanted to be let in and wanted me to open the small window.

"Open the landing window, Tich," he called softly.

Carefully he got two old water butts, miraculously putting one on top of the other under the window, without making too much racket. He got his hands on the window sill and, with me pulling, scrambled into the house. In return he scrumped his mother's apples from the orchard, put them in a bag and left them in the hedge for me to collect as I went out in the morning. He must have told his brother that help was at hand if he too got locked out for that was not the only occasion when an illicit entry was made. How their Mum slept through it I'll never know. Or did she?

As previously mentioned, I had been sent here to supervise a gang of girls. When I arrived there were only about six but this number soon increased to twenty. Again, this was to be a clearance job, as the trees had been felled some years before, the branches and waste being left to decay. Brambles and weeds abounded. Once amongst the tangle the only means of finding the girls was by shouting, when they would stick a bill hook in the air. My job was to ensure that all was cleared according to the Foreman's plan. It was a very large area and the girls worked in pairs, starting from the outer edges and working inwards. As a clearing was made a fire was lit. Sometimes it was very dry so great care had to be taken to ensure that the fire did not 'run'.

"I'm on fire! Help" yelled Eileen.

"Smother it!" A horde – or so it seemed – descended on her, rolling on the ground and rolling on her.

"Smother it," I said, "not her."

A spark from the fire had set her dungarees alight and she had not noticed it until she felt it! Her dungarees were taken off and stamped on to make sure they were safe. Eileen was left looking scared and embarrassed in a pair of scanties!

"Good thing men don't work up here," quipped Cherry.

"It's not them I'm worried about," said Eileen.

"How do I get back to the digs like this?"

"Who's going to see you?" asked one of the others.

"You can go the long way round through the woods.

Anyway, you can put your dungarees back on, and we'll walk behind you to hide the hole in the back-side of them."

There were blackberries galore, bigger than I had ever seen before. We each had our fill, so within a few days were hacking them down mercilessly, as they'd lost their appeal.

"I'll turn colour if I have any more," said Cherry, "especially as there is usually a blackberry pie for our meal in the digs!"

At some time in the past many large beeches had been felled then, for some reason, left. These were to be sawn into smaller pieces with a cross-cut.

"Saw them! I can't even reach the top," moaned Muriel, who was not much taller than me.

"Stand on something," advised her friend, going in search of a log.

"This isn't very steady," said Muriel, stepping down. The saw was then above her head!

"It wouldn't 'alf make a smashing comb," laughed Eve.

"I know," said Paddy, one of the taller members of the gang, "get on my shoulders."

Bending down, she allowed Muriel to get on her shoulder, but no sooner had Muriel and her partner got the saw in when they collapsed into a heap, amid much laughter.

Those beeches really were big and neither wooden nor metal wedges, hammered in, were effective in keeping the cuts open to stop the cross-cuts 'binding'.

"Let's give 'em best," suggested Cherry, tugging at her saw.

The Foreman was sent for.

"I reckon they'll have to be blown to pieces, dynamited. B— they are."

Next morning we arrived to find three men boring holes in the giant trunks, ready for the insertion of the explosive.

"You lassies must get under cover and lie flat until it's safe. We'll call 'Take Cover' twice, then there'll be an interval of about twenty seconds before the big bang."

Soon the cry 'Take Cover!' came. We flung ourselves to the ground, covering our heads with our hands against the flying chunks of wood.

"ALL CLEAR!" This happened several times until the once lordly beeches were but scattered chunks of wood.

"Get the girls to collect as much as they can and stack it up," I was instructed. Actually it was too far flung and we later learnt that a piece had landed on the roof of a cottage, 'frightening godly people out of their wits'.

To get to the site I had to leave by 6.30 a.m., first crossing a field in which there were cows or bullocks grazing. Many a time I wasted precious minutes sitting on the stile, plucking up courage to pass them, whistling to get them to turn round so that I could identify their sex and then deciding if the longer way round was the safest. The rutted tractor path up the wooded hill was hard going, but especially treacherous when it was muddy.

At that time in a morning it was fairly dark, for the early rays of the sun had not penetrated through the dense forest. It was eerie. Often I was startled by a pheasant, flapping off as I disturbed it. However, I came to enjoy the solitude of the wilds, except when it was raining, for the air was fresh and invigorating.

Part of my responsibilities was the welfare of the gang, reporting anything serious to our Divisional Welfare Officer. One day there was a deputation awaiting me.

"We're not trying to make trouble, Tich, but none of us likes working with –." She scratches her head a lot, and we think that it's lousy."

I found an opportunity to get her on her own and tactfully asked if she would mind if I looked at her hair. It was easier than I thought it was going to be, for she admitted that she had been uncomfortable. Our Divisional Welfare Officer had to know. Instead of dealing with it herself she advised me to get in touch with the District Nurse. Easier said than done. Furiously cycling from place to place I finally caught up with her.

"I'm terribly busy," she informed me, "at least two births imminent. Home births. Can you deal with it yourself? Get some sassafras oil. Comb the hair through with that. Paraffin will do if you're not near a flame!"

Where was I to get sassafras oil from? I couldn't get into town until the weekend owing to the very limited bus service and it was only Tuesday. It would have to be paraffin! So I told the girls, "No curlers tomorrow. Scarves for your heads. No smoking if you don't want to go up with a bang!"

Armed with a small tooth comb, which my Mum always insisted that I carried, I went to the main site. Here I begged some paraffin in a tin, carefully climbing the mile or so up the hill, trying not to spill any. There were a few grouses about 'rat's tails', but one by one every girl submitted to being sat down on a tree stump in a clearing and having her hair combed. Not one but several were affected. On Saturday, I got the sassafras oil and every day for almost a week I combed and was combed. It became quite a joke, despite the fact that they had to wash their heads every evening, often in cold water. At last, the 'all clear'.

A letter from the village parson was delivered at the cottage for me, explaining that the members of his congregation felt that they ought to offer the strangers in their midst some entertainment. The girls were not very keen but a gesture had been made, so I felt that at least I ought to accept.

My path lay across an enclosed area in which a bull often grazed. Believe me, I'd have won any cycle race! Arriving somewhat hot and bothered from my exertions, I was ushered into a large room, against the walls of which sat both women and men, either knitting or talking.

"May I introduce Miss Williams of the Timber Corps?"

Nods from many heads.

"Do sit down, Miss Williams. Make yourself comfortable."

I was directed to a large armchair but, sensing all eyes upon me, I was feeling anything but comfortable!

"Now," said the person, "as Miss Williams is our guest she must choose the first hymn."

Hymn! Think, Mavis, think!

I was so taken aback that I could only think of one.

"Eternal Father," I managed to say.

In the corner of the room was an old pedal organ.

Sitting by the woman organist was an older gentleman whose job apparently was to pump air into the organ.

Occasionally he either forgot, or didn't pump hard enough, for no sound came out. Nothing daunted the organist started where she had stopped, so the singers were often a line ahead. I thought this very funny, but the regulars must have been used to it and didn't bat an eyelid. Several hymns were sung in similar vein until sandwiches and tea were served, after which we sang some rounds.

"Bring the others along next time," I was told.

I managed to have a word with the parson and tactfully pointed out that the girls were of various faiths or not, and that this type of 'entertainment' was not really suitable. Apologising, he said, "Oh dear. I hadn't realised that. We'll do better next time."

It took some persuasion to get the girls to go for I couldn't promise them an exhilarating evening. This time, instead of hymns, sea shanties and rounds were sung. I dared them to notice the organ, but it was more than difficult to smother the inner laughter. It was meant well, but the girls would much rather play darts or sing round the piano at the local inn.

After about three months of poor food and difficult living conditions I was taken ill. I struggled on for about ten days but was finally forced to go home where I stayed for nearly a month.

I was transferred to another division – the Southern Division which embraced Cornwall, Devon, Somerset, Hampshire and surrounding counties.

It was Cornwall for me! Here I was to spend two very happy years.

Overleaf: Bathing in a forest stream in Cornwall – our only means of washing.

7 To Cornwall to become a Forewoman

A small holding, three miles outside Bodmin, was to be my next billet. The working site was some distance away so it meant a very early start. The Foreman had arranged to meet me outside a little inn in Dunmere, the nearest place on the road to the wood. We then began a journey up a single-track railway, walking on the sleepers, pushing the bike on the narrow side path. This proved to be quite a feat, for the rails were dazzling and I had to stretch my short legs from sleeper to sleeper.

Mr. Briggs, the Foreman, told me that it was a relatively new operation, very little having been done to date.

"Here you will be in charge of both civilian workers and Timber Corps girls. We have both sexes working here, most of the civilians being locals. Does that prospect daunt you?"

If it did I couldn't say so, could I?

"There is a great variety of work – felling, pit-props, charcoal-making, logs for firewood, loading railway trucks, hauling by horse, and we must clear as we go, for it is to be replanted."

Charcoal-making! I'd never done that!

The railway ran through a valley, flanked on either side by dense woodland, and through which ran a clear, sparkling stream bubbling over rocks and pebbles below the railway bank. Nothing but trees! Most of it seemed to be oak coppice run wild, interspersed with silver birch. At last we came to a small clearing where wooden huts were being constructed from the trees already felled. There were only four

Timber Corps girls, a few men and a civilian gang of women who came by lorry from a nearby town. For a time I did all the office work, but also had to scour the surrounding district for 'digs' as more and more Timber Corps girls arrived. Billets in town were hard to get but I knew that the girls would be far hap-pier if they had something to do in the evening.

The civvy women were the toughest bunch I had ever met, their language making my hair stand on end. I was soon to realise, however, that they had hearts of gold, if accepted for what they were. They would bring food for the Timber Corps girls whose digs were not too good, give pocket money to the younger girls who found it difficult to manage, help anyone who was in trouble such as paying the fines of two girls who had been caught riding without lights. Their language may have been colourful but the standard of honour was high. Most of the Timber Corps girls got on well with them except two, who persisted in segregating themselves. These two girls would never enter the canteen but would demand to have their tea outside.

"Who the b– hell do they think they are," demanded Marge, the tough, fat leader of their gang. "Not good enough for them, I suppose."

One very wet day, with the mud up to my ankles, I arrived at the canteen hut to find the door barred by two of the heftiest women on the site.

"Come on in, Miss Tich."

"What's going on here?" I demanded.

"Those two. Those snorty bits. Those are not coming in. If we's no good enough for them on a fine day, we's no good enough on a wet day."

Needless to say it didn't happen again as the lesson had been learnt.

A young boy of about fifteen accompanied his mother to work for some reason. He was always to be found at the top of a tree. Any visitors or strangers were spotted quickly, and it was a good way of gathering the gang together, for when tea was ready he would shout

'Grogo!" which was then passed from group to group. Tools were downed and workers emerged from all directions to empty the boiling billies despite having to scoop out flies and sundry other insects.

One lunch-time all the civilian women workers disappeared; so did the tall Irish foreman. Lunch over, the Timber Corps girls returned to their work. About three o'clock a commotion was heard – loud singing, shouting, raucous laughter. Into the clearing came the foreman, holding a girl up on either side, the rest following, rolling, falling, crawling on all fours, laughing and shouting and very, very, drunk! Until their lorry came they lay about in the hut while the foreman went to sleep. Soon after this incident the foreman was transferred and I was promoted in his place.

Now the prospect was daunting! In charge of the 'whole works', I had to learn fast. I was fortunate in having the help of a well-educated man who had fallen on hard times. He was very patient and proud of his ability to make good charcoal. Sticks which were either too thin or too crooked for pit-props were cut into pieces about two feet long on the Porta-saw and thrown into a heap near the kiln to be packed. These kilns were in two tiers, the top having to be rolled off while the lower tier was packed. Before packing, a 'fire-place' was made in the centre with oily rags covered with twigs and small pieces of wood. Around this the pieces were carefully packed as tightly as possible starting from the outside, round and round lengthwise – a skilled operation.

When the first tier was packed the second tier had to be man-handled and logs thrown in for the loader to pack. The lid was then heaved on, the joins round the lid and tiers being carefully sealed with mud and sand to prevent the entry of air which would make the fire burn too fiercely and so spoil the charcoal. Four pipes spaced equally round the circumference of the kiln led from the outside almost to the centre – 'the fireplace'. The kiln was ignited by pushing a lighted oily rag tied to a long stick through the pipe facing the direction of the prevailing wind, usually south-west. When two or three kilns were in action the heat was unbearable and the smoke from the chimney choking. Mr. P– had to gauge when to close down a kiln after twelve to twenty hours burning by sealing off the pipes and the chimney. When they were cold the top was heaved off, men and girls climbing inside to bag the contents – a dirty, dusty job, especially as we had no proper washing facilities. Occasionally the kiln had been left to burn too long, so that nothing but ash was left.

Sam P– lived in a little hut in a field on the edge of the wood but we never found out exactly where. It was constructed of wood with a corrugated tin roof so we were told. The nearby stream was his only source of water and a Primus stove was used for cooking, though often he made a fire outside. He slept on a camp bed. This explained his permanently grubby clothes and his gaunt appearance, with sunken cheeks and no teeth. The girls collected money and gave up some of their clothing coupons to buy him a new shirt and tie. He was thrilled to bits to be invited out — and turned up complete with teeth which, unfortunately, he had difficult in keeping in place. His glass of beer suffered, as did his dignity. Oh yes, he had some dignity despite his living conditions and his appearance. He worked hard. He was a lonely man.

In complete contrast was Arthur B–, a well-fed, pampered man who was employed to do odd jobs. There were plenty but Art could never find them! Saws and axes had to be sharpened regularly, harness repaired, huts strengthened, sticks collected for the billies; in fact, anything. But, if there was a job to be done, Art was never to be found. His excuses were boundless, for he was always doing 'something else', somewhere else.

"I reckon we'll have to erect a stake and tie you on a long rope to it," one of the more outspoken said to him one day. "Then we'd know where to find you."

"I'm always about," he replied amicably.

"About, maybe, but about where? You're never here when we want you. Where do you go?" asked Norman.

"Here and there," he said.

"More there than here, I reckon."

The questions didn't ruffle him one little bit. He was delegated to lighting the fire and making tea three times a day, so his disappearances were fewer.

A Measurer arrived, and shortly another Ganger, twice my size in every dimension, but very efficient. Women worked besides men – felling, sawing, stacking, cutting logs by hand or on the Porta-saws, packing kilns, and hauling wood to the sawing ramps. Some of the finest workers were the gypsies, who brought their horses for hauling, staying until one job was finished, then moving on. Batty, the oldest, oozed beer when he sweated, but was always fit for work despite his nightly 'soak'. Every night he was to be found in the Cranmere Arms chatting to the locals.

"I supplussed the Yanks are on removers, couldn't sleep a wink last night."

"Ne'er mind, Batty me 'andsome, swill it down."

"Swill what down? This 'ere stuff dissembles pregnant water. I ruddy well diffuse to drink more. S'welp me god, damn stuff 'nuff to give one the squinsees!"

"Ow's owd Charlie goin' on Batty?"

"Oh 'im. 'E be snuffed out, 'e be. Wouldn't 'ave been susprised, but he ne'er diffused a meal. Doc man said 'e 'ad squinsees, but I reckon 'e died of ammonia. We 'ad to 'ave an increase on 'im, 'cause the Pooleese said, and 'is brother from Dorch 'ad to come to notify 'im, poor old b–. Ne'er found no dibbins though. Kept all 'is persissions in a slash round his middle. No fool, 'e weren't."

Going to 'ave another, Batty? Be 'e still workin' in them there woods?"

"Aye. Still stankin' poles for them there maidens. All ruddy oak coppice, crooked as 'ell. Not e'en a ruddy succymore. S'welp me God. Disgrace I calls it. Them there maidens look like ruddy prosticutes in on'ly their ruddy breast plates. Feel like getting dispended some days, 'stead of retiring to work."

"Who's drivin' your 'osses now, Batty?"

"My Jimmy and Benny. Right proper lads, they be. That there other lad, mazed Norman I 'ad to push. Goes round sellin' Funkum balls now. Got to 'ave all the 'osses there termorrer, 'cause our little Miss Borse is goin' to reduce me to the Pressed Reporter."

"Time, Gentlemen, please."

"'Night, Batty."

"'Night, me 'andsome. 'Ope there'll be no ruddy removers to-night."

Tractors were in short supply, but we did have one Fordson, which took over when it was too slippery for the horses to haul uphill. Later we were to be the proud possessors of a D2 and a D4 caterpillar tractor. It was very hard work getting the props away, for there was no way out of the wood except along the railway line. The small train would leave a couple of trucks in the morning empty and collect them full of props in the evening. These had to be heaved into the waiting trucks, the larger ones rolled up two poles – known as skids – and dropped over the top, to be loaded according to size and stacked neatly by the loaders.

The trucks were pushed in front of the weary little train until a siding was reached. Often the girls would cycle up the narrow track at the side of the line, talking to the driver. If their balance wasn't too good they toppled down the bank but were saved from rolling into the stream by the brambles and undergrowth.

At this time the evenings were quite light when I returned from work. After having a meal I went out to help the landlord in the fields driving the tractor while the men piled on the hay. It was here that I was introduced to the custom of 'making the hay sweet'. When all the hay from a farm has been stacked in a rick, a young man was supposed to kiss a young woman. I did not, of course, know of this custom, but thought it queer when I was left to throw the last of the hay on top, while they looked on grinning. As soon as I had pitched the last fork-full of hay there was all hell let loose as the farm lads tried to surround me, their intentions now more obvious. One girl

v. four men – I hadn't a chance. I ran for my life, but was caught before I reached the safety of the house.

"Give us a kiss, maid," a fresh-faced young labourer demanded.

"Not a chance," I gasped struggling, as my arms were pinned to my sides. The strength of the lad! A whacking big kiss was planted on my cheek. The hay had been made 'sweet'.

One night one of the cows kept up a constant mooing, and sleep was impossible.

"Is it ill?" I asked.

"No, no, me dear, said Ron, "it be time for mating."

That evening I was given a stick, told to stand by the gate and whack the cow if it turned the wrong way. I didn't like cows! Needless to say I held the stick at arms-length.

"Won't 'urt, me dear," I was encouraged, "just give it a tap now and then."

The cow was loathe to go in the right direction, several times pushing its way through the hedge back into the field. To encourage it my landlady ran ahead of it calling, "Come along, me pretty," and was several yards ahead before she realised that the cow had turned back. Eventually, we arrived at another farm two miles away. The farm was on a bend in a narrow lane.

"You better go stand round that bend," I was advised. Why, I wondered.

Peering, I could see Ron and the farmer leaning over the gate guffawing.

"Go to it, Fred."

They probably thought that I was too young to know the facts of life. The cow contentedly returned home without any trouble.

Another evening I thought I would have a shot at riding a horse. Ron and his wife took me into an adjoining field where there was a young horse.

"On 'er then, me dear," said Ron, helping me on.

"Sit up straight now. Get the feel."

There was no saddle so I clutched its mane. He led the horse on a rope gently round the field a few times. By this time there were some onlookers shouting their encouragement. Suddenly, without warning, Ron shouted in the horse's ear, "Go, me dear!" The horse started to gallop. Frantically I held on to the mane, slipping this way and that. There was much laughter from the sidelines! Down I went into the cow pats. Shades of Camp and Judith!

Meals here were very good for there were plenty of eggs, milk, fowls, meat and cream. Breakfast consisted of two or three thick slices of home-made bread, covered with home-made jam, heaped with freshly made cream. Washing and toilet facilities were still somewhat primitive but, by this time, I was used to them.

I had joined an amateur dramatic group run by the Dancing School. Getting to and from rehearsals was difficult, so I got a billet in the town. Here I was to remain for the next eighteen months, being treated as one of the family. Mrs. V– had three boys, the last of whom she had seen off to the RAF the day I arrived. She had always wanted a daughter and treated me like one, introducing me to their friends and considering me in everything they did.

By this time the gang of civvy workers had left for their journey was far too long, especially as petrol was short. Those who lived locally remained. Some had to move to the other side of the valley to begin all over again, making things a little more difficult as my little office was on one side of the valley and the canteen hut on the other! No sanitary arrangements existed but while bushes and trees were available all was well. One day Vicky disappeared into the undergrowth. As usual, the chorus of, 'We know where you're going', started up. After a few minutes we heard cries of 'Help'. There was Vicky, breeches half-mast, running down the hill.

"Adders!" she yelled. "I nearly sat on an adder."

From then on we looked more carefully where we squatted!

Minor accidents were not infrequent – cuts, bruises, stings and burn – but occasionally there was something more serious. One morning a worker came dashing down to the office.

"Lofty's injured her eye," he said urgently. "It looks bad."

We gathered up the First Aid Kit, Ben bringing up the rear with a basin of water. We met Lofty who had started to walk back, face covered in blood and still bleeding. The inevitable tree stump provided a seat for her while we cleaned her up.

"What happened?" I asked.

"I was felling, and a sharp piece of wood struck me. What's the damage?"

On examination we found that the wood had missed her eye by less than a quarter of an inch, leaving a nasty gash. Two of us helped her along the railway line to the road, where we hitched a lift to the hospital. Four stitches were inserted, while Lofty held on to me as they sewed.

Some weeks later one of the men arrived, holding one very bloody hand in the other. A billhook had hit a knot, bounced off and sliced his finger. I decided that I must use a tourniquet to stem the flow. Just as I was about to apply it he swayed, then fainted at my feet. Another journey down the railway line to hospital!

The worst accident was that to the tractor driver. As the hail had come from the top of the hill we didn't know what to expect. On the far side of the hill which was being cleared lay Boysie in a crumpled heap. He had been hauling trees when the cable had snapped and whiplashed, catching him round the body. He was unconscious. Someone was sent to the nearest 'phone – down the railway line – to summon a doctor. He was lying in deep mud and must have been getting cold, but how did we get him down to level ground? Alf had a good idea. He brought one of the home-made ladders and as much clothing as he could find to pad it. Carefully Boysie was lifted on to it and the hazardous journey downhill made. After about an hour a doctor arrived, took one look at him and said, "Hospital. How?"

Down the railway line! Poor chap must have had a very bumpy, uncomfortable ride, as he was carried on the ladder. The sleepers were irregularly spaced and from time to time he had to be lowered while his bearers changed. The waiting ambulance took him to the hospital, but as that was full he was sent home. Fortunately no lasting damage was done.

8 Work and Play

Most Timber Corps girls by this time were being housed in camps with all 'mod cons' and recreational facilities. We were taken by lorry to visit one where a dance had been arranged. I happened to dance with a reporter from one of the local papers. A day or so later he arrived at the site to interview me and some of the gang. In due course a long article (see Appendix) appeared and I wrote to thank the Editor for his interest. Replying, he very courteously invited any of us to go to his home for the weekend, for a day or just for a bath! Two of us went, to be graciously received and welcomed. His home, after some of our digs, was sumptuous. So began a friendship which lasted many years.

He was a lonely man, in his fifties, without family and recently left a widower for the second time. Having read the report he decided that here was something useful he could do to lighten our lot. Almost every weekend he organised a Concert Party or hired a band, found a hall, paid for transport – in order to entertain us. Alternatively, he would take a party into town to shop and then entertain them to supper.

Parades were held in many cities on a given day to boost morale. One such day was 'Wings for Victory' in 1943. Together with the Navy, the Army, the RAF, the WRNS, the ATS, the WAAF, the Land Army, the Nursing Services, The Home Guard and many other organisations the Timber Corps were invited to take part.

We'd had no training but our image was at stake, so we must look as smart, disciplined and drilled as the Services. There certainly was not a suitable spot, flat and clear, in the woods to practice and the

Our first March Past, Bodmin 'Wings for Victory', May 1943.

girls were too far-flung in digs to meet in the evenings. In front of the canteen we sorted ourselves into sizes, height-wise – the smallest in the front, three abreast. I cast my mind back to Training Camp and Hercules, the PT, the marching, the barked commands.

"Stand up straight. Feet together, by the left. By the left," I commanded, "QUICK MARCH!"

What a shower! Lefts were mixed up with rights. Three abreast became two abreast or even one on her own.

"Halt! What a mess! Line up again. Sort your left legs out. By the left, QUICK MARCH!"

The result was the same, again and again and again. However, we were all determined to get it right and spent most of every break persevering.

"It's all very well, Tich, you bawling, 'Left, right. Left right.' What happens when we reach a stump? The rhythm goes," Mona said.

"Marching horizontally on a hillside makes me feel as though one of my legs is shorter than the other," added June. "It won't work."

"Oh yes it will. C'mon, let's line up again," I encouraged.

From now on the commands became, "Left, right. Over, right. Left, right. Left right. Over, right," as stumps impeded their path. The only trouble was that the length of stride obviously varied, and while the command may have helped at the front those at the rear had to do their own negotiating. It was hilarious for the civilian workers who had sat watching the many failures and delighted in yelling 'Over' every time a girl reached a tree stump, whether at the front or at the rear of the group. It all became very confusing.

Despite the difficulties of trying to march in wellies on a muddy hillside, of trying to avoid protruding tree stumps, at the parade we were smart, disciplined and drilled. At the command, "Eyes right," every head turned simultaneously as a VIP took the salute.

In 1944, on a similar occasion, we were fewer in number and needed less practice. However, on the morning of this parade I had raging toothache.

March Past in Bodmin High Street 'Salute the Soldier', April 1944. Lumber Jills bringing up the rear.

"Take a few aspirins with you maid," advised Mr. V–.

I slipped more than a few into my hip pocket. When the parade came to a standstill every so often I slipped one onto the offending tooth. The pain was stilled temporarily, but the end of the two mile march couldn't come quick enough for I gradually became more and more 'woosy'. The dentist had been alerted by my landlord so quickly obliged by removing the tooth without anaesthetic.

People who had come in from outlying districts to see the parade had not seen Timber Corps girls, neither had some of the locals. As a result of our first appearance on parade the local chemist asked if he could come to the woods to photograph us at work and play. From then on he took a fatherly interest in us and 'slipped us the wink' when he'd had some cosmetics in. We never went short!.

Meanwhile work in the woods went on, the beautiful valley beginning to look bare and untidy. Piece-work was now the order of the day. We had to measure out square chains for the fellers fighting our way through the remaining undergrowth, crossing numerous streams, marking out the boundaries by felling a tree across, often paddling barefoot. The girls sawing pit-props and paid by the inch were now earning a lot of money as were the fellers and haulers. But my Measurer, my Ganger and I were on a fixed wage. We became the 'poor relations'!

The streams provided a means of cooling off during very hot weather, so often during the lunch hour the girls departed to one stretch, the men to another, to have a dip. At least once a week the girls came armed with toilet bags and towels and sometimes a bathing costume, for in one part of the wood there was a natural deep pool. Soaped down we jumped into its clear, but very cold waters, our only means of a bath. Sure we could bath in front of a fire at our digs from time to time but this was far more fun and exhilarating. It was refreshing and we could dive from the small rocks, and swim in the deepest part. However, word somehow must have got round that as well as lumber jills in 'them there woods' there were also 'water nymphs'!

Pluckie, my Measurer, on my right; Renée, my Ganger, on my left.

"Do you get the feeling that we're being watched?" asked Renée as she was rubbing herself down.

"Can't see anyone," answered Doris.

"Come out whoever you are," she yelled at the top of her voice.

From behind some trees emerged three soldiers – American soldiers!

"What the devil are you doing here?" demanded Doris.

"Watching you, of course," said one, jaws going twenty to the dozen.

"Gee! What a gorgeous sight," said another.

"We're no tourist attraction" stormed Renée.

"That's what you think, honey."

Gradually, of course, the conversation became more friendly, but we were careful on all future occasions to keep our costumes on.

My landlord was an attendant in the local mental hospital, in the town.

"I've got an idea, but I'll have to get permission from the 'Super'", he informed me one evening.

"Can I hear about it?" I asked interestedly.

"Well, I've been thinking about all you maidens bathing in that there pool in the wood. You'll catch your deaths. There are plenty of baths in the 'Big House' and they'm not used in the evenings. The Super might let you use them."

"Hot water?" I asked.

"As much as you want."

The prospect was pleasing. Very pleasing. Luxury at last!

"Don't say anything to the girls yet," Mr. V– advised.

I could hardly keep the good news to myself during the three days it took to get the Super's approval.

So, one Wednesday evening we met in a group outside the massive, iron gates set in the surrounding high wall, armed with all the toiletries we could muster. Mr. V– produced a very large bunch of keys, opened the gate and led us up the drive. Down bare-tiled corridors we marched, every door being unlocked in front of us, then locked behind us. Finally, we reached a large room in which there were twelve baths, six on each side.

"I'll lock you in, give you half an hour, then come and let you out. Enjoy yourselves."

As soon as the door closed, we began to strip. The stone floor was cold to our feet, but by that time the atmosphere was warm and steamy, and we couldn't wait to jump into that lovely hot water.

"Sheer luxury," sighed Vicky as she submerged.

"Bliss. Sheer, sheer bliss," added Lofty as she soaped her long limbs.

Here we luxuriated for the best part of half-an-hour, adding more hot water as that in the bath cooled. A few had managed to get some bath salts, others some talc so that cold, bare room smelt like a perfumery.

After half an hour we heard a loud knock on the door.

"You'm maidens finished?" Mr. V– shouted. "Have your three-pence ready."

The door was unlocked and he stood there with his cap ready to collect our payment.

"Here's your threepence, and worth every penny," said June contentedly.

The procedure of unlocking and locking doors was repeated, and so began a regular ritual.

Timber Corps bath night, from a drawing done by Pluckie.

On the whole we were a very happy and united gang, with a great team spirit. The few quarrels soon resolved. So that we could have a lasting record of our camaraderie and of those happy days, we decided to compile a magazine, inviting both Timber Corps and civilians to contribute. Once again our friendly Editor came to the rescue and presented us with an ancient but fairly efficient duplicating 'jelly'. The Measurer, Pluckie, a very talented artist, drew some of the incidents that had occurred, with remarkable likenesses of the girls concerned. An old typewriter was borrowed to type the articles and poems. However, before it was ready we were split up.

Two such contributions are as follows, the first written by myself:

Come on girls, let's rally
To the call of the forests green.
Come on girls! Don't dally
We're so proud to be seen
On a winter's morning, frost on the ground,
Birds chirping blithely, though no food to be found.
Stepping out boldly, heavily laden
With an axe, a hook and a saw.
Green sweaters, cream shirts,
Black boots, dungarees of beige,
Hair in a turban,
Wind in our face.
Every day, on our way
E'er the stars leave the sky
Into the depths of the forest,
Into the mud and the mire.
Maybe singing a song,
Maybe telling a tale,
We're light-hearted, for
There's a job to be done.
Sweethearts in khaki,
Sweethearts in blue,
Fighting for peace,
Their ultimate due.
We're proud of them, but
They're proud of us too.
Proud of their girls with a man's job to do.
Proud that we're fighting hand-in-hand
For the right to live in a far better land.
The call of the woodland, an open-air life.
Countries at war in a world of strife.
We've accepted the challenge
We'll see it through
Together with women in khaki and blue.
We're doing our share,
We'll try to do more
As very proud members of the Timber Corps.

Another, written by Pluckie, and which embodies the idealism of the age, is entitled 'Youth's Aim':

And what are we fighting for? Do they know
This tired work-worn Youth, aged prematurely
To maintain a life that should be spent
In adolescent joys?
Maimed by the crashing bomb, blinded
Blasted from dugout home and shelter.
Dying, disabled, name upon name
Of countless thousands.
Mothers lonely in bereavement,
Dreaming of well-beloved sons. Husbands
Whose brief and happy days
Snatched from the jaws of war
Have ceased for ever.
We, who are left, will reap where these have sown
Strive to prevent another million
Killed by our false philosophy.
We shall disown all greed for wealth and power
Causes known
As creators of war and strife.
And in this great new world each human life
shall play a part.
That we may build
Lives of contentment
And with gladness filled
Freedom from want
And opportunity.
A lasting Peace
For all security.
Freedom to do, to speak, to work
This is Youth's aim.

We all had our share of boy friends, especially being in or near a garrison town. Monday mornings were almost a dead loss as far as work was concerned for everyone was interested in what everyone else had done during the weekend. One tale was recounted by Myra and Julie. They were billeted on a small-holding outside the town.

In the garden was a large apple tree, the apples too high to pick by hand. Often they had looked at it, even shook it, wondering how they could get at the luscious looking apples. One Sunday morning Myra, already dressed in her 'pink wonder' as she called her dress, said to Julie, "Let's have a go at that apple tree."

"I'm not dressed," June pointed out.

"Never mind that. They'll be back from church soon. Hurry!"

When they went outside they found that the ground was very muddy underfoot.

"Go and get our wellies, " Myra urged Julie, while she divested herself of her pink wonder. Dressed only in undies and wellies she scaled the tree, while dressing-gowned June stood below, catching.

They were so engrossed in their task, that it came as a great surprise when a voice demanded, "Got nothing to wear then?"

One leg over a branch, the other dangling, Myra turned her head to see Jim, their landlord, hands on hips, laughing his head off.

"While you're there, me dear, might as well pick enough for all of us. Saved me a job. Mrs. can make an apple pie."

So Myra, in undies – now somewhat grubby – remained up that tree for over an hour!

Talk naturally centred around the weekend's activities – old boyfriends, new boyfriends, who danced with who, who went where with whom, but often some went further afield by hitching. Most of us had become quite adept at it, without showing any leg! Every evening somebody tried, not always successfully, for after the walk down the railway track, when work was finished for the day, the journey into town was all uphill, tedious, tiring and often disheartening when the weather was bad, as in most digs there was nowhere to dry wet clothes. Clad in sou'westers, waterproofs and wellies, looking anything but glamorous thumbs – and smiles – were directed at any passing traffic. Lorry drivers were the most helpful, but often we would have to clamber on top of the load at the back to be blown to bits in a howling gale and hang on for grim death – not very comfortable but quicker than walking. Jeeps were another source of transport, and often as many as a dozen girls would climb in, arms and legs sticking out at all angles.

"Bet you can't guess what we did at the weekend," threw out Eileen who, we thought, was one of the quieter girls.

"Let's have it," said Gladys, somewhat suspiciously, not believing that Eileen could have anything exciting to tell.

"Freda and I went all the way to T–," she said.

"So?" asked Glad.

"None of your lorries and jeeps for us. Nothing so common. There we were at the top of the hill, thumbs stuck out, in macs and wellies, when a large car stopped. A very large grey car. We thought the driver had probably stopped to ask the way. But no, he got out, came round to us and asked us where we wanted to go. We couldn't believe our luck!"

"We were ever so wet," interrupted Freda.

"He said that that didn't matter," continued Eileen, "and opened the passenger door and ushered us inside."

Oh! It was lovely! The seats were so soft and the car purred along instead of bumping."

"Who should be so lucky," remarked Glad.

"That wasn't the end of it though. He said that if we were ready by five o'clock he'd bring us back too."

"Hitching will never be the same again after that," sighed Eileen.

As trees disappeared we knew that the day was fast approaching when we would be transferred elsewhere, for by that time men had started replanting. A petition to the Divisional Office, requesting transfer as a gang, went unheeded. Few by few the gang dwindled. My Ganger was promoted to sub-Forewoman to live in the lap of luxury in a purpose-built camp. There were lots of tears and promises to keep in touch as fond farewells were said. Then it was my turn to go! My spirits were already low, but sank even further when I looked at a map to find where I was going. Dartmoor! With great sorrow I packed my bags, and bade *au revoir* to my second home.

Stinging nettles waving green
In Jim's orchard seen,
Wilson's appetite as usual
Could not brook the law's refusal.
So, Sunday afternoon with Jeff
She planned the most stupendous theft.

Julie wasn't really dressed,
But Myra, togged up in her best
Thought her 'Pink Wonder' to protect
She'd take it off and so bedecked
In cami-knicks and Wellington boots
She up-ed the tree and downed the fruits.

(Drawing by Pluckie)

9 Redundant on Dartmoor

My billet-to-be lay off the beaten track – nothing new! I had to catch a branch line train from one of the larger towns. The stations were tiny, each station-master being his own signalman, porter and guard. A station-master's house, within yards of the railway track, was to be my destination. Amazingly, my new landlady was young, with a child of three. The house was extremely clean and furnished in a modern style. Water was laid on but there was no form of lighting, except for a couple of oil lamps, so it was 'a candle to light me to bed' again.

I was soon to find that my landlady was very house-proud, to the extent that visitors were few and far between as they never felt comfortable. I never knew where to sit, for if I sat in an armchair, the cushion was swiftly whipped from behind me, and I wasn't sure if the chair would go too – cushions were constantly being plumped up! Consequently, I was to spend most of my evenings in my bedroom, writing to all and sundry by candlelight or reading – until the candle burned away. When I had time to explore, I found that the nearest village consisted of about twelve houses and a general shop. The Post Office was some distance away up a very steep hill, but fortunately there was a post box near my billet. While I was here

Opposite above: Civilian workers in Cornwall, including gypsies, 1943.
Opposite below: 'The Gang', Cornwall, 1944.
Back row, from left: Paddy, Muriel, Brenda, Nancy, Myra, Vicky.
Front row, from left: Pluckie, Julie, Myself, Muriel, Peggy.

there was a heavy fall of snow so I was literally buried until the lorry could run again. No buses touched the village, the last train returning from town on a Saturday at 6.30 p.m.!

Our friend the Editor promised my Ganger and I, before we left the area, that he would make arrangements for us to return to his home for occasional weekends. I was some ten to fifteen miles away and Wendy almost as far. However, on a Friday evening a taxi would arrive at the door of my digs. At that time, a taxi could travel only so many miles from its home base. I can't remember just how many miles was the rule, but I had to change into another taxi which would be waiting when the first taxi reached its allotted limit; it was a masterpiece of organisation. Lying stretched out on the back seat was most relaxing, even though it was dark, as inside lights were not allowed because of blackout regulations. We lingered in hot baths and had as much as we could eat, cooked to perfection by his housekeeper. Sunday evening the procedure was reversed, the second taxi always waiting when the first arrived.

Had it not been for these weekends I would, no doubt, have been very lonely, for on the site there were no women workers, just local men most of whom were medically unfit for the Forces and generally illiterate. I found this out when one day I had to go out with the lorry, leaving a note pinned to the office door saying that it would be back in time to take them home. When the lorry returned the site was deserted for they had started to walk back. Wages were often signed for with a cross. However, for all their academic shortcomings they were the most mannerly and considerate bunch of men I had met. Logs were always plentiful for my office fire as were cups of tea.

The wood was some distance away from the road. Italian prisoners-of-war were building a small railway line into the wood, stretching for nearly two miles over some very boggy ground. I saw a horse almost up to its neck in mud and the valiant efforts of the men to rescue it with ropes and planks. Wood was loaded on to trailers which were drawn behind the small engine but, due to movement in the track on the treacherous ground, trailers often came off the rails and had to be reloaded covered with slimy mud, the men knee-deep in it.

The only other woman I saw was the lorry driver who from time to time delivered logs to isolated villages. As I sometimes went with her to unload, I learnt that the lanes were very narrow and winding. Handling a big lorry was no joke, but I saw Stella get in and out of some very awkward places with a lot of patience and effort. Frequently she had to drive over ice-bound lanes with no chains on the wheels, often making no progress. Then we had to get out to throw ash under the wheels to get a grip. Taking all the men back to outlying districts was quite a mammoth task and meant driving down lanes which were hardly visible in the snow. I admired her nerve.

"I've got a dreadful pain in my side," I said to Stella one day while loading.

"Gawd! You can't be ill here," she replied, "you'll never find a doctor. He's rarely found in the same place twice."

My landlady noticed that I was not eating my food, and I had to admit that I often felt sick.

"You can't stay here. I've my baby to think of," she soon informed me. "You'd better pack your bags."

At home an appendicitis was diagnosed as the probable cause of my pain but after a week I was so much better that no operation was needed. A further week was spent at home then, as a change, a transfer to Exmoor! At least I didn't get to Princetown though I was very near it!

The tide of war was turning in favour of the Allies. It made me wonder what the future would hold and for how much longer I would be a lumber jill. Would life seem tame after life in the Timber Corps? At least, it now seemed as though there would be a future. Maybe this would be the last posting.

10 Exmoor: My Last Posting

Last billet or not, it was little different from my others, for again it stood on a road, a mile or so from the village. But, at least, it looked a big house. Climbing roses clad the white-washed walls while the front garden was neatly laid out to flower beds. My new landlord, a solid man, flanked by several other men, was waiting for me. Almost a guard of honour!

"Welcome, missie," he said in a broad Devon accent, "we're all most pleased to meet you. All the lads here. Not often we see a new face."

Enthusiastically, they all pumped my hand and raised their caps.

"Obliged to meet yer. How de do?"

Weather beaten faces smiled and grinned, some embarrassed by it all, but I could not help smiling to myself for I realised that they'd probably never heard of the Timber Corps and had come to size me up. Perhaps they had expected an Amazon. If they had they didn't show it, but no doubt they had a good natter afterwards. Courteously I was shown inside to meet my landlady – a plump, homely-looking woman stood by a table loaded with home-made goodies.

"Sit ye down, lassie," a strong Scots accent invited, "ye must be hungry."

Gratefully, I tucked in, feeling that here I would be made comfortable. I was not wrong.

"I'm real sawry the wee boys are not here to meet you, lassie," Mrs. M– apologised, getting up from the table. "Ye'll want to see your room."

It was huge, furnished with solid oak, bright cotton curtains at the window, and the thoughtful touch of a vase of flowers beside my bed.

"Come ye down when ready lass, and sit by the fire."

After a wash in the inevitable basin I did just that, although the weather was not cold. I got the impression that they had lit the fire just for me.

I was introduced to a young man.

"This is our Charlie. Now, Gordon, come and meet the wee lass," she cajoled another.

"Good boys, they be," said Mr. M–. These were their sons. When she had said 'boys' earlier, I had visions of bare knees, short trousers and scuffed shoes! Imagine my surprise when I saw two hefty, suntanned, young men. Charlie was the taller of the two, but even 'wee Gordon' was at least five-feet-ten, with dark curly hair and blue eyes. Those eyelashes! In contrast Charlie was fair, his blue eyes piercing, his smile revealing white, even teeth.

Gordon shook my hand gently, said 'Hello' shyly, and flopped into an armchair. Charlie, however, was out to impress.

"Hello, Miss Williams. I say, I like your uniform. Not bad, what's in it too."

"Call me, Tich," I suggested, surveying him from my lower level.

"Now why should I do that? It's not very complimentary for a nice young lady is it?"

"You call me Tich," I reiterated. "Then I can call you Lofty."

"Well done, lassie," his mother laughed. "That'll take him down a peg or two."

"OK. OK. You win," Charlie conceded, "Tich and Lofty it is."

Conversation flowed easily after this banter and, although most of it was about the day's work, I found it interesting and was more than happy to be included in the family.

"No doubt you'll be tired lassie, and wanting your bed," said Mrs. M–. "These wee lads o' mine would keep ye up all night blithering."

"Tell you what," said Charlie, as I sipped a hot cup of cocoa, "It's quite a walk to the woods from here. I'll take you on my bike."

"There's a good wee laddie," smiled Mrs. M– proudly. "That'll save the lassie some time."

"Goodnight all," I said as I prepared to go upstairs.

"Goodnight Miss Williams," was the general reply, except for Charlie who rose to open the door.

"Goodnight Tich. Sleep well," he said with a twinkle in his eyes.

After a very good night's sleep I was wakened next morning by, "There's a wee drop o' water, for ye, lassie," said a smiling Mrs. H–, putting the enamel jug on the washstand, then drawing the curtains.

"It's going to be a bonnie day for ye."

A very good breakfast awaited me and the pack of sandwiches I was given seemed enormous.

"I'm ready, Tich. Get a move on," yelled Charlie from the door, "Your carriage awaits."

I had had visions of riding on the cross-bar of Charlie's push bike, but no, there outside stood a motor cycle. Travelling in style!

"Jump on, then. Sling your bag over your shoulder and hang on to me round the waist."

Hang on! I had to for it was worse than a circuit at Silverstone: – there were more bends! My feet only just reached the rests – or my toes did – so I was almost flung off several times. I hate to think what the girls thought when they saw their new Forewoman arriving in such a dishevelled state.

"Hello, Miss Williams. Come into the office," welcomed the Foreman. A real office!

"I'll introduce you to the girls later. First I'll take you round the site. Jump in," he invited, indicating a little van.

It was a very large site with groups of men and girls working at various points.

"Apart from clearing, we deal mainly in telegraph poles and pulpwood," he explained. I'm sorry that your billet is not nearer. When possible I'll run you back." I could hardly believe my luck. Good billet and transport!

After lunch, eaten in the office, I was left to my own devices visiting various groups. The tall, stately trees were felled mostly by the men, then lopped, topped and peeled by the girls. This was a very sticky job when the trees were newly felled because of the oozing resin, and a backaching job if they had been left to weather. They were then cut to regulation size. No 'shoulder' loading here, for the transporter had a hoist. The only real difficulty was rolling them into a neat pile. Pulpwood of certain sizes was also peeled and packed when dry.

I suspected that I had been sent here more to supervise the welfare of the girls than to control the operation. The girls were all very friendly but a few nagging worries emerged:

"My boyfriend's a prisoner of war."

"My husband was killed when his plane crashed."

"I think I'm going to have a baby."

"My new dungarees haven't arrived and these are in rags."

It was here that I met Olive, who was to become a loyal friend for forty years.

Except for my early morning rides and the amorous advances of the irrepressible Charlie, life for me was comparatively peaceful. Determined not to wobble I pressed my legs against the sides of the motor bike after that first morning, but for my trouble got some very nasty burns as I touched the twin exhausts. Evening jaunts were soon abandoned for Charlie took too many detours and stopped far too often!

VE day was announced amidst great jubilation and to celebrate we were granted two days leave. Where to spend it? Many girls lived at too great a distance to go home. Barnstaple was the nearest town offering any entertainment. Everyone else must have had the same idea for the streets were thronged with people celebrating, in their own ways, victory in Europe. Guest and boarding houses were already full. Then we saw a hostel run by a religious organisation and made for that.

"Yes, we have some room at the top of the building," we were happy to hear, "Are you all God-fearing girls?"

Of course we were! When it suited our purpose!

After the outside rejoicing, the atmosphere was stern and sombre but we had somewhere to sleep. Up the bare stairs we climbed until we reached the top. A large room had been made in the space under the roof, sloping down steeply on two sides. At last, I had an advantage in being small – I could stand upright! Some, in fact most, of the others had to bend in order to avoid bumping their heads on the beams. There was electric light and in one corner a small bathroom with warm water. Under the slopes of the roof were camp beds so we literally crawled into bed as they were so near the floor.

"Not what you'd call luxurious, but better than nothing," whispered one of the girls.

"You are to be in by 10 p.m. We make no exceptions and lock the door promptly at that time. A bell will wake you at 7 a.m. Breakfast is at 7.30 a.m. Stand behind your chairs when you come down. The hostel is closed from 9.30 a.m. until 6 p.m. When you come in there is to be no noise in your dormitory and no smoking." With this the Warden departed, leaving us to unpack.

"And good luck to you all!" Ruby threw at her disappearing form.

"Blimey! What's this? Borstal?" demanded Eileen.

"Oh, shut up Ei. Let's get out. We've got a couple of hours to paint the town red," retorted her friend.

We tiptoed down the stairs and let ourselves out. Bells were ringing, hooters hooting, anything that could be banged, banging and people singing, arms round each other, pent-up emotions showing at last. Curtains had been drawn back, lights piercing the darkness after over five years of enforced black out. My ganger and I decided to find a Dance Hall if we could. It was packed, couples dancing 'on the spot'. The air was alive with happiness and excitement. For a couple of hours we sang and danced and fraternised.

"We'd better get out of here, Emma," I said. "It's after 9.30 p.m. and I've not seen any of the others."

"Bet I know where they are," answered Em.

So we did a round of the pubs, dragging reluctant jills away from the revelries which would go on all night. More than one was un-steady on her feet for what beer there was had been free and flowing. All but one were rounded up and she would have to take her chance. Just before the stroke of ten we crept in, pushing the unsteady girls up the stairs in front of us, imploring them to be quiet. Getting them undressed and into bed was difficult, for one wanted to sing and another to dance. The singer we gagged with a scarf while the dancer was forcibly restrained by sitting on her! To add insult to injury the 'missing' member was fast asleep, undisturbed by our antics. Apparently she had been feeling unwell so had returned to the hostel early!

Clang! Clang! Woke most of us with a start, for at the open door a large metal hand-bell rung vigorously. No way were we going to get a lie-in. Having all had a swill we went down the stairs together, marching single-file into the dining room, large and austere. Dutifully we each stood behind a chair trying hard to suppress giggles. A small, sombrely dressed lady appeared from a side door to take her place at the head of the table.

"Good morning, ladies. We will now say Grace before partaking of the food which has so bountifully been bestowed on us....You may now sit."

In silence we sat while meagre portions were 'bestowed upon us.' A large Bible appeared. We ate in time with the monotonous voice of the reader.

"Please stand behind your chairs, ladies. We will now give thanks for that which has so graciously been bestowed on us. Remember that you must be out by half-past-nine."

"At least they mean well," said Louise as we escaped up the stairs to get our outdoor togs.

"It's not their fault if we're just a bunch of heathens," remarked Jo.

That day passed all too quickly, but the following morning was a blueprint of the first, except that our behaviour was a little more reverent, as we now knew the procedure. At 8.30 a.m. the lorry arrived, as had been arranged, to pick us up. Work didn't come easily after the two-day break.

"Och. It's good to see you back," greeted Mrs. M– that evening. "We missed ye, lassie. Come and sit ye down and tell me all about it."

A whacking big meal was put in front of me, but somehow I just couldn't eat very much.

"Is there something troublin' ye, lassie?" asked Mrs. M– kindly.

"No, I don't think so," I replied, not admitting to feeling sick. "Maybe I'm just tired."

"Get ye up to your bed and I'll peep in later."

I slept well, but the queasy feeling persisted. The ride to the site with Charlie didn't do anything to make me feel better.

Olive came into the office to have a chat, for she had spent her two days in London. Suddenly she broke off in mid-sentence and stared hard at me.

"Are you all right Tich?" she asked.

"Just feeling a little bit queasy," I replied.

"You're going yellow, I swear."

"Yellow! Don't be daft."

"You are you know, especially your eyes. Look in the mirror."

Sure enough when I did look I realised what she meant. The whites of my eyes were streaked with yellow and my face was also tinged. I looked at my arms and partly stripped. I was yellow. That to me meant only one thing – jaundice!

"Fetch Jack," I asked Olive. She must have told him for when he came he took one look at me and said, "It's a doctor for you, my lad."

"If I'm ill I'd rather go home."

"I'll see if I can get the van to take you to Taunton," he said full of concern.

When I went to collect my things Mrs. M– was kindness itself.

"If you're ill, lassie, get ye to bed. I'll look after ye." Knowing how hard she worked cooking for the labourers, feeding the hens and looking after the three men I felt that I couldn't inflict myself upon her, so insisted on going home.

That was to be my swan-song, for after some weeks at home I agreed to my release.

My story as a Lumber Jill now is told. It has been almost fifty years in the telling. It tells of a life, of how 'the other half lived'. It tells of fun, friendship, hardship and kindness, of the fight to win a future. It tells of the camaraderie of groups of people thrown together by force of circumstances in united effort towards a common goal. We were on the land. Our Land.

Lumber Jills going to collect pit-props, Lanhydrock Saw Mill, 1945.

Postscript

The end of the war did not mean there was no more work to be done in the country's forests. There was, but it was work of a different sort which demanded mental rather than physical skill. With the amount of timber which had been required for various uses during war-time our stocks in this country were very depleted, some woodlands having completely disappeared, leaving ugly, untidy scars on the landscape.

So, a comprehensive census of what was left was quickly organised by the Research branch of the Forestry Commission. It was hoped that all the depleted private woodlands would be assessed. To this end, many Timber Corps women were employed as Civil Servants. Their job was to survey private woodland throughout the country. Several groups spread out across each county armed with six-inch maps, searching out all woodland over five acres. The information they had to record included the species, age and condition of the remaining trees, the size of areas which had been felled and the acreage of each and every species. All this meant a lot of book work and accurate recording, the women again having to work in all weathers on sometimes difficult terrain. The results were tabulated and analysed, the whole operation taking two and a half years to complete.

On completion, two women were transferred to Silviculture (the branch of Forestry concerned with the cultivation of trees) where experiments were carried out, in the field, to determine the best conditions for the growth of particular species. For instance, larch races were studied at different elevations at Savernake in Wiltshire and on Snowdon in North Wales. Genetics – the study of heredity and variations in species – was another branch of research. Seeds were collected, their methods of propagation being the aim of the study. Other women became 'beat' clerks within the Forestry Commission's own forests. A 'beat' is a specific area of forest under the charge of a Forester.

The Control Commission in Germany also recruited ex-WTC women as clerical staff to Forest Officers organising timber supplies and re-afforestation. In this country replanting went on apace, but this was often done by men.

Dunmere in Cornwall was replanted immediately and is now, after some fifty years, restored to its former beauty, full of bluebells and primroses in Spring.

On release many women returned to their pre-war jobs as shop assistants, hairdressers or clerks while others married almost immediately as serving boyfriends returned or prisoners-of-war were freed.

Me? Well, I had the opportunity to go to Germany but, though it was a tempting offer, I realised that apart from a Matriculation Certifi-cate I had no other qualifications. My parents, having nothing but their old-age pensions on which to live, advised training for a 'safe' job with a pension at the end of it. So I applied and was accepted for the Emergency Teacher's Training Scheme, entering Exmouth Training College in March 1946. My main subject was Physical Education. After a year of concentrated training I was one of two students to be given the opportunity to go to Homerton College in Cambridge for specialist training.

Starting in a tough London school in 1947, after five years and marriage I moved first to Buckinghamshire, then Bedfordshire, and finally Suffolk, teaching mainly Physical Education to both boys and girls of secondary age for sixteen years. On the death of my husband I moved to Bristol in 1963 where I eventually taught slow-learners and problem girls over fourteen years of age until my retirement in 1981.

In 1987, in an effort to find 'my gang', I contacted 'Searchline' on Cilla Black's TV programme 'Surprise, Surprise!' Photographs were shown and an appeal made. The response was quite surprising, for I not only heard from nine of 'the gang' but from my landlady's son, a gypsy worker, a civilian worker, and Ruth, my first Timber Corps friend at Culford Camp in 1942.

The Lumbergirls
Happy warworkers near Bodmin
Doing Man's size job

"Gr-o-o-go–" This seemingly foreign and untranslatable word called out at various intervals of the day by a strong female voice is one of the most popular with the girls of the Timber Corps. It means anything that one can eat or drink, so its popularity is understandable. It echoes through the green foliage and the lofty woods and is passed on by the girls until it reaches the last person in the remotest part of the coppice. Surely and not too slowly girls trickle in to the 'base', where they have their own canteen and wireless.

At this particular working centre in Dunmere Woods, near Bodmin, the eleven girls who make up the TC complement there are one happy gang. They are all bronzed with the summer sun, and all looking healthy and content with life. In green jumpers and calf-coloured riding breeches with their hair blowing in the wind, they have settled down to work as hard (and perhaps even harder) than some of the men whose jobs they have taken over. Their ages range from 18 to 22, and they hail from all over the country – Liverpool, Halifax, London and Bristol are only a few of the distant towns and cities they live in. But this part of the country seems to suit them very well; in fact, when girls do settle in to work in the woods of Cornwall, they rarely want to go elsewhere. All the girls in the Corps are, of course, mobile, and this sometimes entails moving from one place to another many times in a year, but on the other hand, if it is a large wooded area that is being felled, they may be stationed in one place for a long period.

A typical day in their life is started when then report from their various billets in Bodmin at the 'base' around 7 o'clock. The base is an already-cleared area, with a timber hut as an office and a similar building with a galvanised roof as a canteen. Miss M. Williams, 22 years old, is the forewoman, and the first thing on arrival is to check with her. Then in twos and threes the girls make their way along the old mineral railway line to their work. At Dunmere this consists of cross-cutting and sawing wood into various lengths for pit-props for the Welsh minefields. After the felling of the trees on the slopes, horses are used to tow them down, and then they are passed over to the TC girls for cutting.

The length of a pit-prop is determined by the type of wood and the straightness of it. The wood most commonly found here is oak, with a few beech and birch interspersed. The standard types of props are 3ft., 4ft., 6ft. 6ins. and 9ft., and the classification to different sizes is the girls' responsibility. When a certain amount is finished and given the 'OK', it is stacked on a slope above the mineral railway, and left there until the arrival of the train. The empty trucks are run underneath, the smaller props are heaved into them by the girls; but the larger ones are transported in by 'skids', the official name for the two pieces of wood on which the props roll down. This generally commands the presence of six or more girls. Two at the top to start the logs rolling, two at the sides in case any become stuck, and two are in the truck itself. This once-daily job over, they have a break and then continue cutting till 5.30. By this time they have done a good day's work, and are ready for something a little less strenuous.

An officer for this area of Timber Control says that although the work may seem hard, actually after a while the girls enjoy it, and they seem to be quite at home in Cornwall. In the summer they have had an ideal site for working at Dunmere, with a view that stretches for miles, with endless green slopes of different trees, and below them is the fresh running river, which has been a great joy to all as a place of relaxation after a toiling day in the woods. But, as one girl said, everything in the dry weather is marvellous, but when you have to toil and saw with a heavy raincoat and the wind is blowing in your face it's a different matter! The main point is, however, that all the girls like it, and are agreed that it is a war job worth doing, even if some do want to return to other less strenuous occupations after the war.

In the midst of their work recently the girls found a moment or two to give their views on the Timber Corps.

First to give her impressions was Miss Mary Foster, of Halifax, who before joining up was a sales assistant. She has been in the Timber Corps for three years and thoroughly enjoyed the work. Her 'partner' and girl friend, Miss Muriel (Killer) Berry was also a shop assistant in the same shop in Halifax. Her department had been ladies' lingerie, and as she remarked chopping tree-trunks and handling ladies' underclothing are just as extreme as can be imagined. But she really liked the job, although after the war she looks forward to something a little less energetic.

Further on from the Halifax girls were two very energetic young women sitting stride an old oak trunk cross-cutting it. Laying down their saw, one explained she was Miss Myra (Wils) Wilson, of Redcar, Yorkshire. She was engaged on a cosmetic counter previous to her two years in the Timber Corps. The predominant complaint here was the effect of forestry work on one's hands. "The more careful you are," Miss Wilson said ruefully, "the worse they become, and then this oak coppice stains them and it won't come off for days." But this is only a minor set back, if that, for Miss Wilson's face is the colour of mahogany, and with laughter on her lips, she looked anything but displeased with her job. Nearby was Miss Nancy Brooks, of Newcastle, who had had a little experience in a man's job before she became a TC girl. She was an assistant to an electrician, and joined this particular war job because she thought it more helpful, and added with a smile "much more exciting". Her views were that to become a 'lumber jill' you must have aptitude for the work, and the open air life must attract you. All the girls' views on Cornwall were complimentary, although for a day at home each said, "Everything here could be swopped."

Miss M. Williams, who is a native of Liverpool, forewoman of the girls, said they were the happiest gang she has ever worked with, and to illustrate this is the poem composed by the girls themselves about their job:

> Blondes, brunettes, tall and short,
> From London, Lancs., and Yorcs.,
> Whoever comes to us they find
> They've left their worries far behind.
> Though work is tough and hands are raw,
> We're the happiest gang in the Timber Corps.

These girls take a pride in their work, and they are doing a most important war job, and even when peace comes wood and timber of all sorts will be in urgent need for all our bombed cities and for industries, which used to receive imported wood previous to 1939. The Timber Corps will be busier than ever then, and the girls perhaps busier still.

We must remember this, so that when we see the not very familiar badge of a pine tree surrounded with the words 'Timber Corps', surrounded with a crown on a Land Girls' beret, we should know the wearer is one doing a man's job, in a man's time, and for mankind's sake.

Also published by Ex Libris Press and uniform with the present book:
LAND GIRL: *Her story of six years in the Women's Land Army*
by Anne Hall   *144 pages; Price £4.95*

Ex Libris Press publishes a wide range of books in the fields of history and countryside. Please write to ask for our free illustrated catalogue:
EX LIBRIS PRESS,
1 The Shambles, Bradford on Avon, Wiltshire, BA15 1JS